STUDIES IN ECONOMIC AND SOCIAL HISTORY

This series, specially commissioned by the Economic History Society, provides a guide to the current interpretations of the key themes of economic and social history in which advances have recently been made or in which there has been significant debate.

Originally entitled 'Studies in Economic History', in 1974 the series had its scope extended to include topics in social history, and the new series title, 'Studies in Economic and Social History', signalises this development.

The series gives readers access to the best work done, helps them to draw their own conclusions in major fields of study, and by means of the critical bibliography in each book guides them in the selection of further reading. The aim is to provide a springboard to further work rather than a set of pre-packaged conclusions or short-cuts.

ECONOMIC HISTORY SOCIETY

The Economic History Society, which numbers around 3000 members, publishes the *Economic History Review* four times a year (free to members) and holds an annual conference. Enquiries about membership should be addressed to the Assistant Secretary, Economic History Society, PO Box 70, Kingswood, Bristol BS15 5FB. Full-time students may join at special rates.

STUDIES IN ECONOMIC AND SOCIAL HISTORY

Edited for the Economic History Society by Michael Sanderson

PUBLISHED TITLES INCLUDE

OTHER TITLES ARE IN PREPARATION

Children's Work and Welfare, 1780–1880s

Prepared for
The Economic History Society by

PAMELA HORN

MACMILLAN

First published 1994 by
THE MACMILLAN PRESS LTD
Houndmills, Basingstoke, Hampshire RG21 2XS
and London
Companies and representatives
throughout the world

ISBN 0–333–60200–5

A catalogue record for this book is available from the British Library

Printed in China

Contents

Acknowledgements

I should like to thank Dr Michael Sanderson for his generous help and guidance. His encouragement has been of great assistance.

P. H.

The author and publishers wish to thank the following for permission to use copyright material:
Manchester University Press for material from W. B. Stephens, *Education, Literacy and Society 1830–70* (1987), pp. 322–3.
Every effort has been made to trace all the copyright holders, but if any have been inadvertently overlooked the publishers will be pleased to make the necessary arrangement at the first opportunity.

Editor's Preface

In recent times economic and social history has been one of the most flourishing areas of historical study. This has mirrored the increasing relevance of the economic and social sciences both in a student's choice of career and in forming a society at large more aware of the importance of these issues in their everyday lives. Moreover specialist interests in business, agricultural and welfare history, for example, have themselves burgeoned and there has been an increasing interest in foreign economic development and Britain's role in the wider world. Stimulating as these scholarly developments have been for the specialist, the rapid advance of the subject and the quantity of new publications make it difficult for the reader to gain an overview of particular topics, let alone the whole field.

This series is intended for undergraduates, sixth-formers and their teachers. It is designed to introduce them to fresh topics in the curriculum and to enable them to keep abreast of recent writing and debates. Each book is written by a recognised authority and authors are encouraged to present their subjects concisely to a wider readership without being either partisan or blandly disinterested. The aim is to survey the current state of scholarship, not to provide – in the words of the first editor – 'a set of pre-packaged conclusions'.

Studies in Economic and Social History has been successively edited since its inception in 1968 by Professors M. W. Flinn, T. C. Smout and L. A. Clarkson and has expanded with the growth of the subject. In particular there is now a concern to include more social history and more non-English themes. The editor both commissions new titles and receives unsolicited proposals. In this way the series will continue to reflect and shape the ongoing development of this rich seam of history.

MICHAEL SANDERSON
General Editor

University of East Anglia

1 Introduction: 1780–1850s

(i) Differing perspectives of childhood and child employment

At the end of the eighteenth century two opposing philosophies underpinned contemporary attitudes towards childhood. The first, and most widely held, stemmed from a belief in the innate sinfulness of all humanity and the consequent need to curb and control youthful high spirits. Habits of industry must be inculcated since 'idleness' was equated with moral weakness, and each child had to be trained so as to ensure that the correct values and beliefs were absorbed.

For the upper classes this disciplined approach meant an emphasis on drudging memory work and the 'culture of the mind' [Cruickshank, 1981]. For the lower orders, it led to concern to promote early employment, either paid or unpaid. The educational writer and reformer, Mrs Sarah Trimmer, reflected these ideas when she declared in 1787 that it was 'a disgrace to any Parish, to see the Children of the Poor, who are old enough to do any kind of work, running about the streets ragged and dirty'. Likewise the Philanthropic Society, set up in 1788 to rescue criminal or abandoned children, regarded 'indolence' as the prime source of evil and 'industry' as the principal virtue. This not only encouraged acceptance of child labour in agriculture, mining, manufacture and, especially for girls, in domestic service but it encouraged the promotion of schools of industry and similar educational institutions in the last decades of the eighteenth

9

century. By 1803 there were around 21,000 pupils attending these schools in England alone and according to Mrs Trimmer, their mixture of labour and learning was 'particularly eligible for such children as are afterwards to be employed in manufactures, and other inferior offices in life'.

A similar attitude underlay efforts to promote Sunday schools from the 1780s. These were welcomed because they instilled the rudiments of religion, morality, punctuality and discipline at low cost, without interfering with the week-day work plans of labouring children or allowing them to spend their one day of leisure in idleness and wrongdoing. Robert Raikes, a pioneer of the Sunday School movement, claimed that it was the disorderly conduct of young workers from a Gloucester pin factory on the Sabbath which had led to his setting up schools in that city. Once within the classroom, the pupils 'entered a new universe of disciplined time', and by 1811 nearly a quarter of all working-class children aged from 5 to 15 were estimated to be Sunday scholars [Laqueur, 1976; Thompson, 1967]. In 1787, Mrs Trimmer enthusiastically described the aims of the sponsors:

> Wherever Sunday-schools are established, instead of seeing the streets filled on the Sabbath-day with ragged children engaged at idle sports, and uttering oaths and blasphemies, we behold them assembling in schools, neat in their persons and apparel, and receiving with the greatest attention instructions suited to their capacities and conditions. [Cunningham, 1991]

Such views were based on a widely held belief that individuals should be encouraged to remain in their 'proper stations' in life [Horn, 1978]. It was an attitude which was slow to die. As late as 1857 Samuel Wilberforce, Bishop of Oxford, claimed there was 'perhaps, too much outcry against children being taken from School early to work on farms', adding that they 'did not want everybody to be learned men, or to make everybody unfit for following the plough, or else the rest of us would have nothing to eat'.

The 'moral Puritanism' characteristic of this approach to childhood was in marked contrast to that put forward in the late eighteenth century by the followers of the French philosopher Jean-Jacques Rousseau and of the English Romantic poets. They stressed the natural goodness and innocence of the young and the loss of these qualities in adult life. It was a philosophy neatly summarized by William Wordsworth:

> Heaven lies about us in our infancy!
> Shades of the prison-house begin to close
>   Upon the growing Boy,
>   But He
> Beholds the light, and whence it flows,
>   He sees it in his joy; . . .
> At length the Man perceives it die away,
> And fade into the light of common day.
> *Ode: Intimations of Immortality from Recollections of*
> *Early Childhood* (1802–4), lines 66–77

For those who held such views childhood was regarded as a separate and distinct stage of life, with its own special qualities, rather than as a time when juveniles were considered almost as small adults who must be prepared for the world of work. It led to children being valued for their own sake and it informed the actions of some of the reformers seeking to improve the lot of youngsters whose existence was particularly harsh, such as the climbing boys recruited by chimney sweepers and the pauper apprentices sent to work in the early textile mills. But its influence was to prove short-lived. In the revival of evangelical religious opinion in the early nineteenth century, it was the older belief in the need to control children's natural wilfulness and to train them in the way they should go which predominated. Although most parents continued to value their offspring, there was nonetheless a 'distinct intensification of adult demands for obedience and conformity' on the part of the young [Pollock, 1988]. Hence 'much that was harmless was forbidden, and much that was pleasant, frowned upon' [Pinchbeck and Hewitt, 1973]. Even in their infancy many youngsters were taught the importance of the work ethic and those who deviated from the desired pattern of behaviour were strongly castigated. In 1851 one writer described the juvenile delinquent as a 'hideous antithesis, an infant in age, a man in shrewdness and vice . . . the face of a child with no trace of childish goodness'.

Throughout the period children (i.e. youngsters under the age of 14) were treated as subordinate members of society, lacking individual rights and under the absolute authority of their parents. In that way an orderly family life was promoted, contributing, it was hoped, to harmony in society at large. This did not, of course, preclude most parents and children from having affection for one another. In working-class families, in particular, the bond between a mother and her offspring could be strong. Only in adolescence did strains begin to emerge between them, and these were often at the children's volition [Sanderson, 1968; Anderson, 1971].

However, this simple societal model failed when parents neglected their role as guide and mentor, or when children were orphaned. Slowly and reluctantly the State began to intervene in certain carefully defined areas to lay down minimum standards of protection and provision for the young. Inevitably these initiatives extended adult supervision and control over the lives of the children, even while they improved their lot in other respects. But there remained a determination in official circles not to interfere in domestic relations so as to intrude upon the 'sanctity of the hearth'. As John Stuart Mill observed at the end of the 1850s:

> One would almost think that a man's children were supposed to be literally, and not metaphorically, a part of himself, so jealous is [public] opinion of the smallest interference of law with his absolute and exclusive control over them.

(ii) The scale and nature of child employment

Between 1780 and the 1850s the need for the offspring of the lower orders to be employed was, therefore, widely accepted. Even the passage of factory and mining legislation in the first half of the nineteenth century was designed to regulate but not to outlaw child labour. Nevertheless its scale and the proportion of juveniles actually at work have long been the subject of historical debate.

To the end of the nineteenth century children formed a substantial proportion of the total population, with the increase particularly noticeable in the late eighteenth and early nineteenth centuries. One estimate suggests that from a low point of 28.5 per cent of total population in 1671, children under 15 comprised 39.6 per cent of the population in the peak year 1826 [Wrigley and Schofield, 1981]. After this, the figure fell back, so that by the 1851 census 35 per cent of the population of England and Wales was under 15; it then rose slightly to reach just over 36 per cent in 1881 [Walvin, 1982]. Inevitably when youngsters were so numerous there was pressure, especially within poorer families, to reduce their period of dependency to a minimum and to set them to work as quickly as possible. Their earnings could play a significant part in raising household income above the level of bare subsistence [McKendrick, 1974]. Hence the comment of a diocesan school inspector in the mid-nineteenth

13

century that the financial problems of Somerset farm workers were so severe that a labourer 'supporting his family . . . on 10s. a week cannot be expected to keep the child at school if that child can earn 3s. a week'.

But, as Hugh Cunningham has suggested, in the late eighteenth and early nineteenth centuries, there were often no jobs available for youngsters to carry out. In rural areas especially the rapid growth of population, coupled with the effects of agrarian reform, led to much child unemployment or under-employment except in districts where domestic industries provided alternative outlets. Regional differences meant that in arable areas like East Anglia work opportunities for children on the land were greater than in the pastoral west. But the evidence indicates that in the early 1800s there was little *regular* employment for young children on farms anywhere. That was especially true of girls but even younger boys had difficulty in finding winter jobs [Cunningham, 1990].

Other historians have also argued that the proportion of children at work was probably greater in the pre-industrial era than during the Industrial Revolution, since at that time children were engaged in helping parents and other family members in agricultural and handicraft activities. Even in 1851 most working children were occupied in 'traditional' tasks, such as farming and domestic service, and in textile production (see Appendix 1).

Elsewhere, as in the small metal trades of the Black Country and Birmingham, industrial change led to an intensification of the existing family-based or small workshop system of production. In many of the Midlands industries when children were not working with parents they were attached to an adult operative and were subject to the irregular and spasmodic work pattern favoured by such producers. It is important to remember that in the 1850s the typical industrial production unit remained the workshop

14

rather than the factory and in London, indeed, few trades were factory-based before the twentieth century. Many youngsters in the capital were thus engaged in casual or 'sweated' occupations, like box-making, artificial flower-making, sewing, running errands, and street vending, often alongside parents or older siblings.

Only in textiles had the factory system and the decline of domestic production clearly changed the nature of child employment by the middle of the nineteenth century, making it more rigorous and regimented. In 1816 perhaps 20 per cent of workers in the cotton industry were under the age of 13, and in 1835, despite the effects of technology in reducing the need for juveniles, they still comprised 13.1 per cent of the workforce. In silk mills, the under-13s formed 29.5 per cent of the labour force in 1835 [Nardinelli, 1990].

It was the expansion of factory production in textiles which made child employment such a controversial issue in the first half of the nineteenth century, both among contemporaries and historians. Contrasts were drawn between the pre-industrial situation, when youngsters worked within the family circle, under the eye of parents, and the new regime, which brought them into the impersonal environment of a mill and required them to meet the demands of power-driven machinery. Even when youngsters worked with other family members, as happened where adult male spinners recruited their own assistants, the speed and nature of the work were determined by the machines and the requirements of the master and his overlookers. In 1807, Robert Southey described a Manchester cotton factory he had visited as presenting a scene worthy of Dante's images of torment should he have 'peopled one of his hells with children'. Southey called the textile workers 'the white slaves of the rest of the world', and comparisons with slavery in the West Indies and the United States were to recur in the factory debate over the succeeding decades [Cunningham, 1991].

It was these conditions that caused E. P. Thompson to write scathingly of the rich who between 1790 and 1830 had described factory children as

> 'busy', 'industrious', 'useful'; they were kept out of their parks and orchards, and they were cheap . . . [The] exploitation of little children, on this scale and with this intensity, was one of the most shameful events in our history. [Thompson, 1963]

Half a century before, J. L. and Barbara Hammond had similarly claimed that during the first phase of industrialization 'the employment of children on a vast scale became the most important social feature of English life'. Although child labour was not an invention of the Industrial Revolution, the changes it inaugurated ensured that for the first time children were important factors in the economic system.

Historians like R. M. Hartwell, however, have maintained that child labour probably peaked during the expansion of the domestic system which preceded the Industrial Revolution and that the widespread use of children on the land could be 'just as harsh and reprehensible, in its extremes, as the employment of factory children in unfavourable circumstances' [Hartwell, 1971]. Clark Nardinelli has also pointed to the 'bias' of some contemporary reports upon juvenile industrial employment, such as the 1832 Select Committee on the Regulation of Factories, whose witnesses were carefully selected so as to present a view of the mills 'as hellish institutions for the destruction of children'. Witnesses to subsequent Commissions and Committees gave a more balanced account. Furthermore, to Nardinelli a concentration on the large number of youngsters working in textile mills could give the misleading impression that that employment was 'part of a typical British childhood. Such was not the case. The employment of children in factories was concentrated in the textile districts of Lancashire, Yorkshire, and Cheshire' [Nardinelli, 1990].

The validity of these conflicting interpretations will be examined in later chapters. Suffice it here to point out that the 1851 population census suggested that 98 per cent of children under the age of 10 did not work regularly for wages, while almost 72 per cent of those aged 10–14 were also either attending school or unoccupied [Stephens, 1987]. Of course, this ignores the many youngsters engaged on a part-time or casual basis who probably did not declare an occupation to the census enumerator and it takes no account of the important role children played in helping to look after younger siblings or in carrying out domestic chores. It is likewise important to remember that age of entry to a first job varied widely, with some children going to work early – although most did not – and with an intermittent employment pattern customary among many.

Boys were more likely to engage in outside work at a young age than were girls, but much depended on a family's individual circumstances. The offspring of widows or the older members of large families were particularly likely to begin earning at an early stage. In the Staffordshire pottery industry in 1861 it has been estimated that more than a third of children aged 8–12 living only with their mother were at work. This compares with fewer than a fifth in the same age group who had both parents or a father only alive [Dupree, 1981]. Again in the Monmouthshire coalfield at the beginning of the 1840s the low wages earned by adult male workers and the high cost of food (partly resulting from the custom of paying wages in kind on the 'truck' system) led to children being taken underground very young. In country districts it was common for pupils to attend school for a few months and then leave in the summer to work on the land. In such circumstances youngsters whose studies amounted in total to two or three years might have these spread over a very much longer period and interspersed with casual or part-time work, before they moved into permanent employment.

The age at which children entered the labour market also varied from industry to industry, and even from district to district within the same industry. In the early 1840s it was common for children in the South Staffordshire coalfield to go underground when they were 7 years of age and general when they were 9. But in North Staffordshire, the competing work opportunities in the potteries kept many from the mines until they were about 13. Similarly, youngsters in the Warwickshire coalfield might begin work at 6, whereas in nearby Leicestershire the thickness of the seams and the weight of coal to be moved discouraged the recruitment of very young children. In that field no child under 7 was at work [Stephens, 1987].

In domestic industries such as cottage lacemaking and straw-plaiting for the hat and bonnet trade, youngsters often began learning the craft at 5 or 6 years, since it was considered that only so could they acquire the skills needed to produce the best work in later life [Horn, 1990]. Significantly, Bedfordshire – a county where both lace and straw plait flourished – had the largest proportion of child workers recorded in any county in 1851, with 16.6 per cent of those aged 5–9 inclusive and 50.1 per cent of those aged 10–14 in employment. It and Monmouthshire also had the highest level of illiteracy of any county at around this time, if measured by the ability of brides and grooms to sign their name on marriage. Hertfordshire, another county where straw-plaiting was common among children, likewise registered a high degree of illiteracy in the 1840s (see Appendix 2).

Employer attitudes were a further factor in deciding the age at which children began work. In mid-nineteenth-century agriculture many farmers considered that a start at 9 or 10 years of age was essential if youngsters were to become efficient adult labourers. But a number of boys obtained their first seasonal employment, helping in the harvest or scaring birds from the growing corn, when they were only 6 or 7 [Horn, 1990]. In the early textile factories, too, owners seeking cheap labour for the simplest manufacturing processes recruited youngsters of 7, 8 and 9. ·

Nonetheless, most children did not have a permanent occupation until they were 10 years or more, even before legislation started to lay down a minimum age. Furthermore, despite the pride of some young workers in being able to contribute to family income, few earned enough before their teens to support themselves. As with the 3s. to 4s. a week earned by child cotton workers in Manchester in the 1830s, the best they could do was to make a modest – though welcome – contribution to total household resources. McKendrick, for example, has pointed out that the 12s. a week earned by poorly-paid male operatives employed by the Gregs at Styal in Cheshire could be doubled if four of their children worked in the mill too. In the case of skilled men earning higher wages, the extra income secured by the children gave their families the means to buy some of the new mass consumer goods coming on the market. This boost to living standards benefited not only the individual family but the economy at large by stimulating demand for goods and services [McKendrick, 1974].

The fact that most youngsters earned too little to support themselves independently is indicated by census evidence. This suggests that the vast majority of working children continued to live at home with family or close kin. Michael Anderson's survey of mid-nineteenth-century Preston showed that 94 per cent of boys aged 10–14 born in the town lived with parents; among non-natives, 88 per cent did so. Of those away from parents, around three-fifths lived either with kin or with employers to whom they were apprenticed or in service. Claims that wage-earning children were willing to demonstrate their independence by moving from the parental home to live in rented accomodation thus appear exaggerated [Anderson, 1971]. Of those living in lodgings, parental death or overcrowding at home probably accounted for a large proportion rather than any display of defiance or self-will. However, this did not prevent contemporaries from lamenting the way in which children threw off family restraint at a tender age. In 1837 the Chaplain of Preston gaol claimed this was a common happening in Preston among youngsters of 12 or 13 [Sanderson, 1968].

One final change in the nature of child employment during the period was the decline in apprenticeship. This had been the traditional form of juvenile labour and training, but its importance diminished during the Industrial Revolution, even before 1813 when Parliament repealed the statute requiring a seven years' apprenticeship to skilled trades. Among the reasons for its diminution was the fact that formerly skilled jobs like handloom weaving were being superseded by power-driven machines served by unskilled operatives. This became especially true for weaving from the mid-1820s. Elsewhere the application of the principle of division of labour meant that unskilled – often child – producers could perform some of the small operations needed to make a finished article. In addition, the concept of apprenticeship, already under pressure in the mid-eighteenth century, was further distorted from the 1780s when Poor Law authorities 'apprenticed' large numbers of young children to cotton factories and even to the mining industry merely to be rid of the burden of maintaining them and to provide industrialists with cheap and amenable labour. In such cases the training given was minimal and, in the textile mills, was frequently of little value in providing the child with the experience needed for a secure job in later life [Horn, 1993]. Nonetheless pauper apprenticeships continued to be arranged in some districts to the end of the period.

They included agricultural apprenticeships for boys in parts of rural Devon, mining apprenticeships in Lancashire and Yorkshire, fishing apprenticeships in coastal towns like Grimsby and Ramsgate and, for those aged 14 and above, there was entry into the Royal Navy and the merchant marine even in the late nineteenth century [Rose, 1991].

Despite such anomalies, however, in certain traditional artisan trades like those of carpenter, tailor, blacksmith and millwright, apprenticeship remained important as a means of regulating entry to the occupation and of providing youngsters with necessary technical knowledge and skills. This involved binding the young worker for a number of years, normally from the age of 14, and regulating his conduct during that time. It also required the payment of a premium and unless this were forthcoming from charity, the youngster's opportunity to enter a 'desirable' apprenticed trade was limited by his family's ability to make such a payment and by parental willingness to agree terms. Among advertisements for apprentices in *The Times* in January 1800 was that inserted by a London tea dealer and grocer, who announced that a 'handsome' premium would be expected from the successful applicant, while the proprietors of a 'Fancy Dress Making Business' promised to take 'particular care' of the morals of their chosen candidate, providing an appropriate premium was also paid. This was likely to be aimed at girl applicants, since by the beginning of the nineteenth century female apprenticeship was becoming concentrated in the fashion-based needle trades of milliner, mantua maker and sempstress of one kind or another [Pike, 1967].

2   The Impact of Industrialization: 1780–1850s

(i)   'Traditional' employments

Despite the increased importance of manufacturing and the associated spread of mass production techniques, in 1851 agriculture and domestic service remained the largest single employers of boys and girls, respectively. In that year over 10 per cent of all males aged 10–14 worked as agricultural labourers or farm servants, and around 6 per cent of all females in the same age group were engaged as general domestic servants and nurse maids. Cottage industries like straw-plaiting and lacemaking were also of major importance for girls, especially in the south Midlands, while a number of boys were occupied in menial services as messengers and errand boys. Shoemaking, too, was still organized on an outwork basis at this time even in areas of major production like Northamptonshire. In 1851 about one in eight of all boys aged 10–14 in that county was engaged in the shoe trade [Stephens, 1987] (see also Appendices 1 and 3).

Many children in these 'traditional' occupations throughout the period worked in a domestic situation, under the eye of family and kin or, in the case of servants, under the direction of an employer who exerted close personal control. Work routines could be arduous but they were also flexible, both in content and duration. Unlike in factories, where a strict timetable was imposed and fines were levied for unpunctuality, in these industries the notation of time was 'task orientated'. Only slowly did that change as factory

22

methods spread into new areas and there was a linked growth of what E. P. Thompson has labelled 'time-thrift' attitudes among capitalist employers [Thompson, 1967]. Hence although the offspring of 'traditional' producers were often expected to lend a hand when needed, the pattern of work they followed was irregular. Samuel Bamford, who started helping his uncle, a Lancashire handloom cotton weaver, in the late 1790s when he was about 8 or 9, remembered spending much of his day on such tasks as fetching milk, going to the well for water, running errands, and 'assisting my aunt at times in the bobbin-winding department'. This last he regarded as a 'piece of bondage' which was compensated for by the freedom he enjoyed when going on errands [Chaloner, 1967]. No such variety was available to his mill-based counterparts.

In agriculture, too, although children might contribute to the family economy from the age of 6 or 7, the tasks they carried out ranged from minor duties like gathering wood and wild fruit or acorns for the pigs, to looking after livestock, scaring birds from the growing corn, stonepicking, weeding, and assisting adults, particularly at the busy harvest season. For girls there were various domestic chores such as helping with the cooking, minding younger siblings, and assisting their mother around the home or dairy. Yet these jobs were rarely continuous and they allowed time for play or schooling, if this were available, as well. Only when children were apprenticed in husbandry, usually at around the age of 12, or were hired as annual farm servants, might a more rigorous routine apply. In Devon in 1808, instances were quoted of girl apprentices of 10 being expected to load dung, scrape the yards and roadways, and drive horses. Such activities, critics claimed, precluded them from acquiring 'those domestic qualifications upon which the comfort of a peasant family so essentially depends' [Vancouver, 1808]. Overall, however, child productivity in agriculture before the age of 15 was low. Significantly most youngsters did not become resident farm servants before the age of 13 or 14, while some younger servants were paid no wages at all. They merely worked for bed and board [Nardinelli, 1990].

But for many village families in the late eighteenth and early nineteenth centuries there was little opportunity for offspring to take up wage labour at all. The Berkshire clergyman, David Davies, lamented that children's earnings in the mid-1790s were insignificant except at hay and corn harvest. He suggested they learn knitting, spinning, or some other domestic craft in order to supplement family income. At a time when mechanization was undermining the profitability of hand spinning such a proposal had little value.

Only in domestic crafts like pillow lacemaking, hosiery, straw-plaiting, glovemaking and shoemaking was the demand for the finished product still sufficiently buoyant to make widespread child employment profitable during the first half of the nineteenth century. In the case of lacemaking, children began to learn either from their mother or at one of the many craft schools which flourished in the lace districts of the south Midlands and around Honiton in Devon. Newport Pagnell in Buckinghamshire, for example, had fifteen lace schools in 1835. They were usually kept by a 'woman in her cottage', whose only justification for acting as teacher was her skill in the craft and perhaps her iron discipline [Horn, 1974]. Academic instruction was negligible and few of the pupils could read or write. Most adopted an awkward bent posture as they worked at the pillows on which the lace was made, and those who did not progress as quickly as required were punished, sometimes by beatings. The intricate nature of the work caused eye strain, especially during the dark winter months. Mary Ann Webb, aged 10, who attended a Towcester lace school in 1841, admitted to being 'tired' after working a seven-hour day: 'my hands ache sometimes; I never feel well hardly ever'.

She earned a shilling a week, out of which she paid 4d. for school fees [*Children's Employment Commission*, 1843]. Yet this meagre sum was valued as a contribution to family income and her attendance at the school was regarded as a necessary 'apprenticeship' for her adult career.

The same was true of straw-plaiting and gloving. Of the plait trade, one commentator observed in 1852 that 'a well-ordered family [could] obtain as much or more than the husband who [was] at work on [a] neighbouring farm' [Horn, 1974]. At that date over a quarter of all female plaiters were girls under 15, although by 1871 this had fallen to just over a seventh.

In both cottage lacemaking and plaiting, child employment only declined finally in the last three decades of the nineteenth century as competing factory products (in the case of lace) and cheap imports (in the case of plait) combined with fashion changes and legislative regulation to undermine their prosperity.

In agriculture, too, a new attitude towards child employment could be discerned, especially when the 1834 Poor Law Amendment Act reduced parish relief payments to needy families and when arable farming became more labour-intensive in the mid-nineteenth century. During the 1850s the number of agricultural labourers and farm servants aged 10–14 increased by over 10 per cent. Often, as in Dorset, adult males were expected to make their children available for work as and when the farmer needed them. In other cases small farmers used their own offspring as an alternative to paying for adult assistance. In Dorset low wages made 'every labourer anxious to send his children out, although near Dorchester this [was] . . . surpassed by the eagerness of the farmer to get them' [Stephens, 1987].

It was in East Anglia that the exploitation of juveniles probably reached a peak, particularly in the fens and marshlands where the public gang system was in operation. In sparsely populated districts where recently drained land had been brought into cultivation on large new farms, much seasonal work was carried out by gangs of women and children brought in from villages and market towns miles away. They were recruited by a gangmaster whose own income depended on the amount of work he could extract from them. About half the members were children under 13. At Castle Acre, Norfolk, where the system was pioneered in the 1820s, children as young as 4 or 5 were being set to work twenty years later. Sometimes they had to walk several miles to reach the farm where they were to carry out stonepicking, weeding, root gathering and other tasks. Much of the work was exhausting and for their efforts younger children might earn as little as 3d. or 4d. a day. Yet, as in the cottage industries, family poverty and a desire to prepare youngsters for the world of work encouraged parents to send them out, despite the adverse effects on their health and education – and sometimes their morals, with illegitimate births common among girls in a number of ganging areas [Horn, 1990]. 'I'm forced to let my daughter go . . . I earn nothing myself', declared one Castle Acre labourer, whose 11-year-old daughter went out with a gang [*Agriculture, Reports*, 1843]. Not until 1867 did legislation prohibit the employment of children under 8 in these public gangs, and make gangs of mixed sex illegal.

It was in these circumstances that J. E. Thorold Rogers claimed that:

> The work of the child in the fields, ill-fed, poorly clothed, and exposed to the worst weather in the worst time of the year was to the full as physically injurious as premature labour in the heated atmosphere of the factory. [Hartwell, 1971]

Yet, if children employed on the land in early Victorian England were expected to work hard, under pressure from their masters and, often enough, from adult fellow labourers as well, it must be remembered that even in the 'ganging' counties most youngsters did not obtain *permanent* posts before the age of 10 or 12. In 1851 only about a fifth of all boys in Norfolk and Suffolk aged 10–14 worked on the land, and although a far larger proportion would have obtained temporary employment, particularly during spring sowing and harvest, they would not have experienced the unrelenting daily routine expected of young factory workers or of another group of 'traditional' employees – the climbing boys recruited by chimney sweeps.

Already in the late eighteenth century the plight of these boys had aroused concern. Many were young paupers apprenticed by the parish authorities; others were sold to the sweeps by their parents for a few pounds. The smallest children were those most favoured since they could more easily climb the intricate network of narrow and crooked flues found in the households of the rich. A tireless campaigner to improve their lot was Jonas Hanway, who as early as 1767 had written that 'these poor black urchins have no protectors and are treated worse than a humane person would treat a dog'. To a Christian concern over their exploitation Hanway added the spirit of a mercantilist, for whom each child had an appropriate 'value'. 'In a well-regulated free community', he declared, 'every child is as much an object of the protection of the state as the adult.'

The youngsters' terror of the dark, suffocating passages through which they had to climb was overcome by 'the pressure of a greater terror below', arising from their employer's mistreatment. Elbows and knees were rubbed raw when they first began work and they were expected to sleep in their master's cellar alongside the sacks of soot. Even the best employers rarely allowed their apprentices to wash more than once a week and most became 'stunted in growth, blear-eyed from the soot, and "knapped-kneed" from climbing when their bones were soft and from dragging heavy loads' [Hammond and Hammond, 1949; Turner, 1950]. Yet despite repeated campaigns on their behalf and much sentimental literature written about their plight, the desire of householders to use their services and avoid mechanical alternatives meant that almost a century elapsed before the trade was *effectively* outlawed.

The first attempt at regulation came in 1788 when an Act specified 8 as the minimum age for apprenticeship and required that every climbing boy be washed at least once a week, sent to church on the Sabbath, and be not compelled to climb a chimney 'actually on fire'. However, lack of an enforcement agency quickly led to its being disregarded and it was not until 1834 that a new Act laid down 10 as the minimum age for apprenticeship. Six years later another Act banned the apprenticing of boys under 16 and prohibited those under 21 from climbing chimneys. Both measures were widely evaded by sweeps and householders, the latter fearing their chimneys would catch fire if they were not swept by the boys. As Lord Shaftesbury pointed out in the early 1850s, sweeps who were prevented from taking young apprentices merely employed children who were not apprenticed. Ostensibly they were recruited to carry the soot bags, but once in the house they were hustled up the chimneys.

In 1864, in yet another attempt to end the practice, a Bill was brought in to prohibit boys under 16 from even entering a house in company with a sweep but, as before, it was evaded. Not until 1875, when fresh legislation required all sweeps to be licensed and expressly imposed on the police the duty of enforcing the 1840 and 1864 Acts, was the abuse finally eliminated [Rose, 1991; Cunningham, 1991].

Although the number of climbing boys was always small – one estimate suggested 550 apprentices and climbers in London in the mid-1780s, while Lord Shaftesbury gave a national total of 4000 in 1854 – their fate has been examined in detail because it provides a salutary warning of the danger of regarding *legislation* alone as a cure for social ills. Only when public opinion had been educated and builders had made changes to allow the safe and easy sweeping of chimneys by brushes rather than boys, did this brutal form of child employment end.

As will be seen, attempts to regulate child labour in other industries followed a similar pattern. What Jocelyn Dunlop has called 'the patchwork methods which ... too frequently, characterize English reform, its hesitation and its extra-vagance occasioned by the fear of spending' was to apply elsewhere. 'The titles and number of the Acts ... are impos-ing', she wrote, but 'if we look at their details, we find that, lacking in courage and foresight, they failed in varying degrees to achieve their objects' [Dunlop, 1912]. Her com-ments are also a sobering reminder that it took more than the efforts of a few heroic reformers like Lord Shaftesbury to rescue the most vulnerable child workers from the harsh demands of the early Industrial Revolution.

(ii) The factory system and textile production

Child employment in textile manufacture long pre-dated the Industrial Revolution, with the offspring of domestic spinners and weavers expected to lend a hand from a very early age. 'Soon after I was able to walk', recalled George Crompton, 'I was employed in the cotton manufacture.' William Radcliffe, the son of a handloom weaver, remem-bered his mother teaching him 'when still too young to weave to earn my bread by carding and spinning cotton, winding linen or cotton weft for my father and elder bro-thers at the loom, until I became of sufficient age and strength for my father to put me into a loom' [Collier, 1964].

Unlike the factories which superseded it, the domestic system allowed a graduated introduction to work, which took account of an individual youngster's capabilities and age. Only from the early 1800s did this change, as the wages of handloom weavers fell and they were required to work more hours to maintain their income. This meant their child helpers could no longer spend part of the day at work and another part at school or engaged in other activities. Industrialization thus began to undermine the working conditions of youngsters employed at home, and this process intensified with the growth of competition from factory-based powerlooms from the 1820s. During the following decade it was widely recognized that weavers were too poor to send their children to school; instead the youngsters had to work to keep the family from destitution [Sanderson, 1968]. As Fitton and Wadsworth have pointed out, it was one of the inconsistencies of the age that while consciences were pricked about children's employment conditions in the close confines of a factory, the sweating that went with the domestic trades was taken for granted [Fitton and Wadsworth, 1958].

It was from the 1770s and 1780s that the use of mass production methods, first in spinning and then in weaving, began to change the pattern of child employment in textiles. As manufacture moved from home to mill, the children moved with it. They became 'hands', to be summoned and dismissed by the ringing of the factory bell and often working under the supervision of strangers. Discipline was severe, being compared by some employers with that of a regiment or a ship.

The first spinning mills were water-powered and were located in remote, sparsely populated districts beside the swift-flowing streams which drove their machinery. Local people were reluctant to enter these unfamiliar structures which seemed more like penitentiaries or workhouses than

30

places of employment. In order to recruit a labour force, therefore, owners had to import workers. Children were considered particularly suitable in this regard, since they were cheap and tractable and their nimble fingers could perform many of the simple processes required. Sometimes, as with Sir Richard Arkwright's mill at Cromford, Derbyshire, they were obtained through advertisements for adult workers with large families. The menfolk were then employed on labouring jobs around the mill premises or on an associated home farm, while the women and children went to the factory. 'Children of all Ages; above seven years old, may have constant Employment', reads one Arkwright advertisment in 1781 [Fitton and Wadsworth, 1958]. In other cases youngsters were imported from town workhouses and orphanages and were 'apprenticed' in the mills, usually until the age of 21. The Poor Law authorities, particularly in parts of London and other populous centres, were glad to be rid of the cost of maintaining increasing numbers of orphaned and abandoned children and they despatched the youngsters like 'cartloads of live lumber' [Cruickshank, 1981; Rose, 1989].

The policy of apprenticing young paupers was long-established, dating back to the sixteenth century. What changed with the Industrial Revolution was the scale on which it was carried out and the distances involved. In 1780 the parishes of St Margaret and St John the Evangelist, Westminster, apprenticed a total of 23 children to various tradespeople in the London area; fourteen years later in a single week in October 1794, they sent 50 youngsters to a worsted mill in Nottinghamshire. Similarly, St Clement Danes, which began sending paupers to the cotton mills in the mid-1780s, as early as June 1782 resolved that 'all those [children] above the age of six . . . be sent to the silk mills at Watford or elsewhere as great savings might be made to the parish'. By the summer of 1805 the parish was despatching

26 young apprentices to muslin manufacturers in Glasgow. Only 6 children in that year were bound to masters in London [Horn, 1993; Rose, 1989].

For the first twenty years of the Industrial Revolution, parish children were a readily available and renewable source of labour for the textile manufacturers. Particularly in the case of large enterprises or those in remote areas, they offered three major advantages. First, their recruitment enabled firms to increase the size of their workforce with comparative ease, thereby removing an important obstacle to growth when other conditions were favourable to business expansion. Second, for bigger concerns the inconvenience of managing large numbers of parish children, with their attendant problems of discipline and maintenance, was more than offset in the early years by the economies they made possible in the use of fixed and working capital. Instead of building cottages for workers at perhaps £50 apiece, businesses could construct an apprentice house to accommodate upwards of 100 children for an outlay of about £300. The fact that they could be kept working for long hours also led to economies in the use of working capital as a more rapid turnover reduced the need for credit. Finally, at a time when there were few jobs for adult males in cotton mills, parish children had the advantage of being unencumbered with families for whom jobs would have to be found [Rose, 1989]. Hence the desire of populous parishes to cut the burden of Poor Law support encouraged the movement of large numbers of youngsters to low-skill tasks in the early factories. Even between 1802 and 1811, when the 'traffic in children' had passed its peak, fifty London parishes despatched over 2000 pauper apprentices to textile producers in the country, with about 1500 going to cotton enterprises. Almost half of the youngsters were aged under 11 when they were sent away [*Parish Apprentices*, 1814–15].

In return for their labour, the children were given food, clothing and accommodation, but the quality of these varied with the character and financial circumstances of the employers. Some, like the Gregs of Quarry Bank Mill in Cheshire, supplied medical care, a modicum of education and leisure facilities. Others, including the impoverished Needhams of Litton Mill, Derbyshire, half-starved and ill-treated their apprentices. In general the worst conditions were in the older and smaller mills but even in the best, working hours were long; 12 or 14 hours a day were common, with perhaps a luncheon break of an hour. In 1816 Sir Robert Peel, a leading cotton manufacturer and father of the future Tory Prime Minister of the same name, admitted that in the early years the spinning mills had been so profitable 'that it frequently happened . . . that the machinery was employed the whole four-and-twenty hours', with the operatives working in two shifts. When this happened, the parish apprentices slept turn and turn about in the dormitory beds. Elsewhere, as with the Arkwrights, who employed no apprentices, young night workers were paid 'extravagant wages' and were said to be 'extremely dissipated . . . many of them had seldom more than a few hours sleep'.

Some of the unskilled tasks performed by the youngest children, such as scavenging, cotton cleaning, and piecing the broken threads while the machinery was in motion, could be dangerous as well as tiring. Small bodies crept beneath unguarded machinery to pick up cotton waste where larger people could not go. However, a momentary lapse of concentration could lead to serious injury, and crushed hands and fingers were common. There was also the noise of the machines to contend with, especially in the weaving sheds, while the dust and fluff of the spinning process harmed the children's lungs and caused stomach upsets and eye infections. The fact that they were constantly on their feet caused the legs of some to become deformed. For those on night work, especially in the fine spinning mills, the contrast between the heated workplace and the chill of a winter morning when they returned home caused chest complaints.

In larger towns apprentices were rarely used except in the case of a few very big firms or those with a bad reputation as employers, because a sufficient supply of 'free' child labour was available. But in all of the early mills juveniles were an important part of the workforce. Even in 1816 about a fifth of the workers in cotton factories were under 13, and at the Gregs' Quarry Bank Mill children accounted for 70 per cent of the labour force in that year [Rose, 1986]. At McConnel and Kennedy's mill, one of Manchester's biggest, 40 per cent of the labour force in 1819 was aged between 8 and 15 [Cruickshank, 1981]. So when reformers debated the use of child labour, they rarely argued that it should be ended. They merely wished it to be regulated in order to eliminate the worst abuses. At this time it was thought impossible to run cotton factories economically without juvenile help. That applied even when better organization and technological change in the 1820s and beyond reduced the proportion of child workers. It was also argued that to outlaw juvenile labour would cause difficulties for parents, who would thus lose an important supplementary source of income. Some employers claimed, too, that factory work could be mastered only if operatives began at an early age.

But apart from providing employment, the factory system affected children in other ways. The emphasis on rules and regulations, discipline, timekeeping, and the need for punishment encouraged similar attitudes to be adopted in schools. The mass production techniques of the factories were applied to education, too, with the setting up of monitorial schools in the early nineteenth century to provide cheap,

34

large-scale elementary instruction. As Sir Thomas Bernard commented in 1809: 'The principle in manufactories and in schools is the same. [It] . . . is the division of labour applied to intellectual processes.' Contemporaries were impressed by the energy and potential for expansion of the mills and they sought to apply such methods elsewhere [Kaestle, 1973].

Factories needed youngsters who were disciplined to obey the dictates of the machine, and a number of owners saw education as an important means of instilling this, as well as of inculcating essential religious and moral values. Some manufacturers set up Sunday schools as a way of exerting 'the social control of the firm over its workers and of raising up young labourers in obedience if not in scientific skill' [Sanderson, 1967]. Others, like Robert Owen of New Lanark mill, saw education as a vehicle for remedying the wider ills of industrial society. Children attended his schools from the age of 3 until they began work at about 10. In the infant school, which particularly established Owen's reputation as an educational innovator, youngsters spent half the time doing simple lessons and the rest amusing themselves, under supervision, in a paved area in front of the institution [Lawson and Silver, 1973].

Yet despite the efforts of the pioneers, large numbers of children employed in factories were debarred by their work and, often enough, by a lack of school accommodation, from obtaining any education. It was partly to remedy this situation that the 1802 Health and Morals of Apprentices Act was passed.

The Act came at a time when public concern over pauper apprenticeship was growing. Already in 1784 an outbreak of fever at one of the Peel family's mills at Radcliffe near Bury had led to a critical report by Dr Thomas Percival and other Manchester medical men, on the poor ventilation, dirt and long working hours experienced by child workers in cotton mills. As a consequence local magistrates decided to cease

35

binding apprentices to any factories where they were required to work at night or for more than 10 hours in the day. Subsequently magistrates in the West Riding of Yorkshire followed that example and gradually public opinion farther afield also changed. In 1802, the parish of St Anne in Westminster resolved not to send children 'to Mills at a distance in the country' [*Parish Apprentices*, 1814–15]. Eventually in 1816 it became illegal to apprentice any parish child from London farther than a radius of 40 miles from the capital. In general that restriction was observed, although elsewhere conditions were less stringent and long-distance migration continued.

The 1802 Act had been initiated by the first Sir Robert Peel, MP for Tamworth between 1790 and 1820. In the late eighteenth century the Peels had employed about a thousand apprentices in their Bury mills and although that total was subsequently halved, Sir Robert claimed he had introduced the legislation because he was unable to ensure his own factory overseers treated the apprentices humanely. He was also influenced by the writings of Dr Thomas Percival and consulted Percival when he was drafting the Bill. It applied only to parish children employed in cotton and woollen mills and did not cover those engaged in other sectors of the textile trade or to so-called 'free' child workers. Not until 1819 did fresh legislation extend the restrictions on hours to all children working in cotton mills, although those employed in woollen, worsted, silk and flax factories were still not protected. It could be argued that the continuing need for child workers in the woollen and silk mills was a major cause of their omission from the 1819 Act [Nardinelli, 1990].

The failure to cover 'free' children in 1802 was particularly important. It came when the growing use of steam power in textile production had led to the industry becoming concentrated in towns, where non-apprenticed children were easily recruited, and when some London parishes were becoming more reluctant to despatch large numbers of young paupers to the country. Cynics could claim that the Health and Morals of Apprentices Act was only passed when the demand for parish labour was already on the wane. Under its provisions night work was prohibited and the apprentices were limited to a maximum of 12 hours' employment a day. In addition during the first four years of apprenticeship a child was to be given lessons in the three 'Rs' during usual working hours, as well as religious instruction on Sunday. A fresh outfit of clothes had to be supplied annually and minimum standards of ventilation and sanitation were required in the mills. Unfortunately, despite its good intentions, the lack of any effective enforcement agency meant that the Act was very unevenly applied [Rose, 1989; Sanderson, 1967]. Like the chimney sweepers' legislation of sixteen years earlier, the conditions experienced by most apprentices still depended largely on the attitude of their master.

Children engaged in the old-style domestic textile industry had worked within the ambit of their family. Critics argued that those kinship connections were lacking in the large new industrial units, even if factory employment brought higher and more reliable earnings than were available under the domestic system. In a seminal work first published in 1959, Neil Smelser disputed this view, arguing that because in the early country mills it was common to hire whole families, with the wife and children then being set to work in the factory, that 'allowed for the presence of a parent with the children during working hours' [Smelser, 1972]. Later, when adult male mule spinners were employed in mills, this process was intensified, since they were allowed to recruit their own assistants and they naturally chose family members for the purpose, since this obviated the need to pay wages to an outsider. Only in the 1820s and 1830s, when further technical change increased the size of the spinning mules and

37

necessitated the use of more assistants, did the arrangement break down. It was at this time, Smelser argued, that pressure for factory reform developed among the adult workers, in an effort to re-establish the old kinship connections.

However, apart from the fact that pauper apprentices, who were an important feature in many early mills, did not fit into this neat model, since they had no kin with whom to work, critics have pointed to other weaknesses in the Smelser thesis. Michael Anderson, for example, has shown that although it was possible for employees to bring their children to work as their assistants in the early cotton mills, on demographic grounds this could have applied to a limited extent only. Even in 1816 a mere 28 per cent of all children engaged in mills in the Preston area worked for kin [Anderson, 1976]. Similarly a sample of Manchester spinners in the early 1830s revealed that 47 per cent of them were under 30. Clearly very few of these would have had even one child old enough for factory work and, given the high infant mortality rates of the period, fewer still would have had two [Anderson, 1971]. 'Smelser's typical picture . . . of a spinner recruiting his own children as piecers . . . may well have been the ideal', writes Anderson:

> It can never, however, have been the dominant pattern at any one time for, given the age distribution of the spinning population, . . . few spinners would *ever* have had enough children of a suitable age to piece for them.

Secondly, many youngsters working in the mills were not the offspring of factory hands. Some, especially in the early days, were the children of handloom weavers who sent them to the mills while remaining outside themselves. Others were the sons and daughters of agricultural labourers and industrial workers, or of widows who were not mill employees. At Cromford, the Arkwrights drew on the families of local lead miners, while at Belper, also in Derbyshire, the Strutts recruited the families of nailers.

The pressure to regulate working hours which intensified from the 1820s was a response to the widening belief that youngsters should have time to engage in 'childish' activities and to attend school alongside their factory labour. By this time, ironically, some of the worst features of mill life had already been eliminated, with parish apprenticeship in textiles virtually dead and general working hours reduced to some degree. Corporal punishment was still used in some factories to instil alertness and discipline and to increase productivity, but more enlightened owners were turning to education as a way of achieving those ends [Nardinelli, 1982; MacKinnon and Johnson, 1984]. A workforce with a rudimentary level of literacy was also becoming more desirable following the greater use of printed rules and regulations – although it must be emphasized that the early phases of industrialization were accompanied by *falling* literacy levels in most of the textile areas [Sanderson, 1968].

Finally, because much factory labour, especially at the beginning of the period, was regarded as *children's* work, it was abandoned when childhood ended. Many workers seem then to have entered another occupation without too much difficulty. Thus about 87 per cent of the males who left Strutt's cotton mill at Belper between December 1805 and July 1812 went into other employment. Elsewhere there is evidence of former factory workers becoming tailors, shoe-makers, clockmakers, blacksmiths, farmers, merchants, hand-loom weavers and labourers. Some moved to adult jobs within the mills and a few even became manufacturers. 'Many adolescent males apparently worked in textile factories until they became old enough to be eligible for alternative employments', concludes Clark Nardinelli [1990]. However, some unfortunates found difficulty in obtaining stable positions in later life. This was especially

39

true of pauper apprentices, and it was on that account that Derbyshire magistrates in the early 1800s resolved never to 'authorize the binding of poor children . . . to cotton mills'. 'We cannot consider cotton spinning as a *trade* . . . the learning of which can secure an independent provision when the apprentice is out of his time' [Horn, 1993].

Females, on the other hand, worked in textile factories during childhood and as young adults, and then, often enough, left when they became pregnant or, occasionally, when they took up another occupation. Some returned to work after the birth of their child, leaving it perhaps to be looked after by a grandmother or older sibling [McKendrick, 1974]. But of 278 females who left the Strutt mill between 1805 and 1812, about 53 per cent gave pregnancy as the reason and almost 30 per cent went to alternative employment. The rest moved away because of dissatisfaction with their work or wages, or for such diverse reasons as leaving the district, going to school, or moving to live with relatives [Fitton and Wadsworth, 1958].

(iii) Mining, metalwork and miscellaneous manufactures

During the first phases of the Industrial Revolution it was the working conditions of children employed in textile production which preoccupied most reformers, even though such youngsters formed only a small proportion of the total juvenile labour force (see Appendix 1). This concentration angered mill owners and in 1840 Lord Ashley, the future Earl of Shaftesbury and a leading campaigner in the factory movement, conceded their claim of bias had some validity. He admitted he had

> long been taunted with narrow and exclusive attention to the children in factories alone. I was told that there were other cases out of the factories equally grievous, and far

more numerous that just as much deserved attention; and I was told . . . I was unjust in my denouncement of the one and my omission of the other. [John, 1980]

It was in the 1830s that evidence mounted concerning the appalling conditions endured by young workers in the mining industry. In 1833, E. C. Tuffnell, a Commissioner in connection with the Factory Employment Commission, interviewed some Lancashire miners and also went underground himself. Shocked by the conditions he found, he declared that 'the hardest labour, in the worst room, in the worst conducted factory, [was] less hard, less cruel, and less demoralizing than the labour of the best of coal-mines'. Four years later another commentator argued that the restrictions imposed by the new Factory legislation were driving young children into other occupations, including mining. One small boy, questioned as to why he was working in a colliery, explained that it was because he was too young to be employed in a mill.

Nevertheless in the general debate surrounding the passage and implementation of the 1833 Factory Act (see Chapter 3), no action was taken to deal with mining, or any other occupation, until 1840. Then Lord Ashley called for the setting up of a Commission to investigate child labour in industries not covered by the factory legislation. He maintained that few people had any idea 'of the number and variety of the employments which . . . exhaust the physical energies of young children, or of the extent of suffering to which they are exposed. It is right . . . the country should know at what cost its pre-eminence is purchased.' The Commission's reports, published over the next few years, shocked public opinion, especially that upon coal mining, which was published in 1842.

Just as technological change in the 1780s and 1790s had created many new jobs suitable for children in textile manufacture, so technical progress had intensified the demand for young workers in other industries, including mining. The introduction into collieries of the tramway and wheeled wagon, or corf, in the second half of the eighteenth century had so eased the task of moving coal underground that it came within the powers of children. Improvements in ventilation, made necessary by the growing size and depth of the mines, also extended the demand for young labour to open and shut the trapdoors used to regulate the air supply. It was in those coalfields where technical progress was greatest that child labour became most widespread [Ashton and Sykes, 1929]. Ironically, too, it was the youngest children, the 'trappers', who were entrusted with pit ventilation and upon whom the safety of the whole mine depended.

Work began at an early age, with some youngsters employed as trappers at 5 or 6, and many more at work by 9 or 10 years. In the South Staffordshire coalfield employers reported in the 1840s that they were 'constantly beset by parents entreating them to employ their children before they are fit for labour, and often insisting upon it as a condition of engaging to work themselves' [Stephens, 1987]. A working day of 12 or 14 hours was common, exclusive of the time taken to travel to and from the pit. Until they were 18 or 20, concludes John Benson, these children worked longer hours than young people in other industries or than the adults who toiled alongside them [Benson, 1970]. For this most received relatively high wages. Nardinelli estimates their pay was 86 per cent higher than the average of other child industrial workers at the age of 10 and over 50 per cent higher at age 14. As a contemporary noted, families 'of *boys* are, amongst pit-people, valuable property, on account of their earnings in the pits. A widow with a family of boys is considered a *catch.*' In such cases the earnings of the children made a substantial contribution to a higher real income for the household as a whole [Pike, 1967; Nardinelli, 1990].

In many districts trappers spent their days underground in solitude and darkness, never seeing daylight for weeks at a time except on Sundays. Some were bullied by older fellow workers, and this was particularly true of the pauper apprentices employed in the South Staffordshire, West Riding and Lancashire fields. There was also a constant danger of accidents, as well as the effects of coal dust on the lungs; explosions, it was said, were 'not infrequently caused by . . . boys neglecting to attend to the ventilating doors or by their being allowed to enter dangerous places'.

When they were 10 or 12 the children became 'putters' or 'hurriers', dragging or pushing the coal from the face to the shaft. In the narrowest seams this could only be done by the young workers crawling along, pulling the corf of coal behind them.

Moral sensibilities were offended by the free mixing of the sexes below ground, not merely among the children but the men and women, too, under conditions which seemed to encourage sexual promiscuity. Complaints were made of the lack of religious training and education of young workers, since few owners attempted to provide schools before the mid-1840s and the newness of many communities in this rapidly expanding industry precluded the existence of older educational foundations. The fact that the children spent their days below ground meant that they had little opportunity to attend school anyway. When action did come it was largely because of unease created by trade union activity and by a realization that the growing use of printed safety rules made it desirable for workers to have a rudimentary reading ability [John, 1980; Sanderson, 1968].

In these circumstances the 1842 Mines Act was passed. It prohibited the employment below ground of all females, and of boys under 10. In 1860 that was extended so that boys could work underground between the ages of 10 and 12 only if they had a certificate of literacy from a schoolmaster.

Otherwise employers had to provide schooling for them for at least 3 hours a day twice a week. The main effect of this was to delay the entry of boys to underground work rather than to promote education. In other cases excluded youngsters went to work as general labourers or in industries like brickmaking which were still unregulated. Nor was any age limit imposed by the 1842 Act on those working *above* ground in mining. In the mid-1860s a Shropshire witness claimed that girls of 7 or 8 were employed on the surface, 'the main criterion being whether they could carry . . . coal-boxes'.

Despite the restrictions on children underground, therefore, even in 1851 more than 24,000 boys under 15 worked in coalmining alone (nearly as many as in the cotton industry) and in Derbyshire, coalfield expansion during the 1850s actually increased the demand for boys. In South Wales, including Monmouth, and in parts of Staffordshire there were allegations of widespread evasion of the restrictions, with colliers' sons leaving school at 10 or younger to go into the pits. The fact that responsibility for the enforcement of the 1842 Act was initially in the hands of a single Commissioner of Mines who had to cover the whole of the coalfields was a further factor encouraging evasion, especially where seams were thin or awkward and child labour especially valuable. There were complaints, too, that the restrictions interfered with a parent's right to dispose of his child's labour as he thought fit – an argument which was advanced also by opponents of factory legislation. Nevertheless, the number of 5–9 year olds employed in the early 1840s remained small. Hair suggests that at about 5000 it was around 5 per cent of all working children in that age group [Hair, 1982]. Only in individual districts like Monmouth and South Staffordshire, where very young workers were relatively common, was the impact of tighter regulations significant.

Throughout the period miners – and their families – were, then, regarded by contemporaries as a class apart, living in their own close-knit communities and rarely attending church. According to the Rev. Thomas Gisborne, who visited miners on the Duke of Bridgewater's workings in 1798, the 'first evil' of pit work was 'the very little education and religious instructions, which their children . . . receive'.

Unlike mining, youngsters under 15 employed in metal-working, pottery and similar trades were of minor numerical importance from a national standpoint even if they were of considerable local significance. None of these industries experienced legislative regulation before the 1860s and most were dominated by adult males, with children acting merely as messengers, helpers and general labourers. Hence although youngsters aged 10–14 comprised about a fifth of the labour force in earthenware manufacture in 1851, the census total of just over 6200 child workers was about a ninth of the number working in cotton manufacture at that date. In 1851, indeed, the total of boys aged 10–14 employed collectively in stone quarrying, slate quarrying, brickmaking, earthen-ware manufacture, iron mining, iron manufacture, and nailmaking was only around three-quarters of that for boys in the same age group engaged in either cotton manufacture or coalmining.

Nonetheless, the conditions many youngsters experienced could be harsh, particularly in some of the metalworking trades carried on in small, badly-equipped workshops or, as in nailmaking around Sedgeley, at forges at the back of workers' cottages. Children began making nails at about 7 or 8 years old and when they reached 10 or 12 were expected to produce 1000 nails a day. Joint family earnings were needed to make a livelihood and, illiterate themselves, the adult workers placed little value on their offspring's educa-tion. Working hours were irregular, depending on adult whim, and many did little at the beginning of the week – celebrating 'St Monday' – and then put in long hours at the end. Discipline could be even more savage than in factories,

45

with young workers in Sedgeley being 'sometimes struck with a red-hot iron, and burnt and bruised simultaneously'. In Willenhall, where children were also widely employed in metalworking, they were described in the early 1840s as being 'shamefully and most cruelly beaten', with horsewhip, strap, stick, hammer handle, file or 'whatever tool is nearest . . . or are struck with the clenched fist or kicked'. By contrast in Darlaston, Bilston and Wednesbury there was no such tradition of brutality [Pike, 1966]. Custom and practice were thus important factors in regulating local conditions of child labour, even without legislative interference. But Linda Pollock's bland statement that, 'Parents have always tried to do what is best for their children within the context of their culture', begs many questions [Pollock, 1988]. To young-sters harshly disciplined by their elders in Sedgeley it was doubtless small consolation to know that this was taking place 'within the context' of communal culture, or to dis-cover that the nailmaking father who hoped he would not have to set his 5-year-old son to work nonetheless added, 'but if I am anyway obligated he must' [Pike, 1967].

Birmingham, too, had much juvenile labour, mostly em-ployed at home or in small workshops. In the city's pin factories the average age of young workers was put at 8 or 9, and of the pin trade generally it was said in the 1840s that pin heading could be done by a child 'as soon as it [acquired] the use of its arms and legs; . . . a clever child might, at five years old, perform the operation as quickly and as effectively as at eight or nine, but could not continue it so long' [*Children's Employment Commission*, 1843].

In Leicestershire and Nottinghamshire girls were widely engaged in hosiery and lacemaking, with 17 per cent of those aged 10–14 in these counties so occupied in 1851. Both trades were still largely domestic, with the family or extended family working as a unit. Even when hand machines were used in large warehouses, kinship ties were retained

46

among the workers. As wages fell in the middle years of the century and parents worked longer hours, similar conditions were forced on the children. Of the offspring of Leicestershire hosiers it was declared that 'as soon as they can ... hold a needle, or are big enough to stand at the wheel, they must either seam or wind'.

Finally in earthenware manufacture, concentrated particularly in Staffordshire, children played an important role. Even in 1861 about a fifth of the workers were under 15, with most boys beginning at the age of 9; earlier in the century 7 had been a common starting age. Among girls, work normally began at 10 or 11. The youngsters were engaged in both potting and finishing, with plate, cup and saucer makers themselves recruiting boys to sweep out shops and stoves, light fires, wedge clay, run moulds and turn wheels, on a subcontract basis similar to that of mule spinners in the cotton industry. Mould running was especially arduous, with young workers required to carry the plaster cast on which, for example, a plate had been made into a hot stove-room, where the temperature was 100–130°F, and the atmosphere was charged with particles of fine clay. Charles Shaw, who began work in 1839 as a 7-year-old mould-runner, recalled that the heat of the stove-room was often so intense that the chimney pipe glowed red. 'To enable the boy to reach the higher shelves in this stove-room, a small pair of wooden steps was used. Up these he had to run for all the higher shelves, say one-fifth of the whole number ... A boy would be kept going for twenty minutes or half-an-hour at a time, the perspiration coursing down his face and back' [Shaw, 1977]. The girls usually worked in the finishing department, painting the pottery or cutting up paper transfers for application to the ware.

A number of children were the offspring or kin of potters but, as Michael Anderson found in the cotton industry of Preston, only a minority of adults in earthenware manufacture

47

ever had enough children of the right age to act as their assistants. In Wedgwood's Etruria factory in 1861 a mere 3 per cent of adult male potters had a son employed in the industry. Research suggests that youngsters aged 8–12 employed in the trade tended to be the offspring not of 'respectable' pottery workers but of colliers, widows and the poor. Equally, it must be stressed that the vast majority of children living in the Potteries had no regular paid employment at that date. Out of a sample of 674 children aged 8–12 living either with both parents or with fathers only in 1861, over 70 per cent had no job, while less than 20 per cent worked in the potteries. Only in the case of widows' children, where family poverty clearly encouraged early employment, was the situation different, with 44 per cent of 8–12 year olds at work (35 per cent in potworks and 9 per cent elsewhere), while 56 per cent were not employed [Dupree, 1981]. Hence even in counties like Staffordshire, where a relatively large number of children worked, the majority of those aged 10–14 had no regular paid employment. Only when family need was great or, in a small number of cases, there were drunken or idle parents was the situation different.

In the discussion on the employment of children in the foregoing occupations – agriculture, textiles, metalwork and so forth – there is an underlying assumption in the literature of contemporaries and subsequent historians that such work entailed many harsh and undesirable features calling out for reform. Yet Neil McKendrick directs our attention to the other side of the picture, namely the enhanced earning capacity of families with working children [McKendrick, 1974]. He suggests that a working family would earn wages in a ratio of 3:2:1 for the man, his wife and his child. Thus a working wife and child could double a man's earnings and such a family with even a few child workers (say three or four) might receive an income three times that of the male breadwinner alone. The implications of this were that a fully employed family, even of the 'working class', could enjoy an income well up into the ranks of the lower middle class, the lesser clergy, shopkeepers and innkeepers. That in turn had an even more powerful implication since it fed into the home demand that was to absorb some four-fifths of Industrial Revolution production. According to McKendrick, therefore, this home demand, on which industrialization depended, did not come entirely from the middle classes but from working-class families. In spite of the low pay of individual members, the collective wealth of such families with working children enabled them to be the effective consumers as well as producers of the output of industrialization itself. The young piecer's nimble fingers and the juvenile coal hauler's straining back helped to win the coins which bought the cotton corduroy breeches, the muslin caps, the beer and baccy of working-class consumption and industrial growth.

3 Rescue and Reform: 1830–1867

(i) State intervention: its scope and limitations

It is erroneous to assume that there were no constraints on juvenile wage labour before the State intervened, through its factory and workshop legislation, to impose such restrictions. Apart from the absence of jobs suitable for youngsters in a number of industries, parental choice and economic circumstances played a major role. In large families while the eldest children might be set to work from the earliest possible age, a different approach could be adopted towards their younger siblings. Again, in the case of girls, these might be kept at home to assist with domestic chores and to look after the younger children, perhaps because their mother was at work or because she was ill or overburdened. As such they were omitted from official employment statistics, even though many were occupied for long hours in drudging toil.

In textiles, technical change had already reduced the importance of juveniles even before effective legislation to regulate their employment was enacted in the 1830s [Nardinelli, 1980]. Quantitatively the statutory controls of that decade had a very limited effect, since relatively few working children fell into the age and occupational categories which were barred. In 1833, before the application of the Factory Act of that year, children under 9 (the age chosen for exclusion) comprised a mere 0.03 per cent of the cotton labour force and 1.02 per cent of that in wool. Only in silk, at 2.7 per cent, were they in any way significant, and silk was exempted from the provisions of the 1833 Act, as was lace, another relatively large-scale user of young child workers. As Hair warns:

> The danger of writing the history of nineteenth-century childhood solely in terms of chimney-sweepers, trappers and . . . cotton-factory piecers and such tiny minority groups – while ignoring the vast majority of children who were in agriculture, in trades, in less dramatic occupations in new industries, at school or at home – is obvious. [Hair, 1982]

The 1802 Health and Morals of Apprentices Act is often heralded as the first piece of labour legislation in Britain. In reality, because it affected a small and very specialized sector of the workforce only – young pauper apprentices – it could more accurately be considered as the end of an older and more narrowly defined system of work regulation which went back to earlier measures concerned with apprenticeship, such as the sixteenth-century Statute of Artificers. Even what might be regarded as the first enactment of the new era – the elder Peel's 1819 Factory Act – was of limited scope, concerning itself only with 'free' children working in cotton mills and lacking an effective enforcement agency. Not until the 1830s did labour legislation begin to be both widely discussed and conscientiously applied.

This change came at a time of political unrest, which culminated in the passage of the 1832 Reform Act, and when steps were being taken to end slavery in Britain's colonies – an object achieved in 1833. In the arguments over factory reform comparisons were drawn between mill workers and plantation slaves, most notably by Richard Oastler in a letter to the *Leeds Mercury* in October 1830. In this he compared the agitation over slave emancipation with the

51

indifference displayed towards the overworking of young children in Bradford worsted mills.

> The very streets which receive the droppings of an 'Anti-Slavery Society' are every morning wet by the tears of innocent victims at the accursed shrine of avarice, who are *compelled* . . . to hasten, half-dressed, *but not half-fed*, to those magazines of British infantile slavery – *the worsted mills . . . of Bradford*!! [Nardinelli, 1990]

Nardinelli has identified four principal pressure groups in favour of factory reform. First, there were the mill operatives themselves and their supporters, of whom Richard Oastler was one of the most prominent. They set up short-time committees to demand a 10-hour working day and used the debate over child labour both as a way of exposing the hardships of the children and as a means of seeking a limitation on the working hours of adults. In the *laissez-faire* atmosphere of the day, any direct attempt to achieve State regulation of the hours of adult males was doomed to failure. But because juveniles aged 10–13 were an essential part of the factory labour force it was hoped that restrictions on their hours would percolate through to the rest. The reformers did not oppose child labour as such, but were merely against unregulated child labour. They judged legislation not by its direct influence on juvenile workers but by its indirect effect on the position of adult males. 'Measures aimed solely at children – such as educational, sanitary, and health provisions – received little or no support from Oastler and his partisans; their specific recommendation for all abuses was always the Ten Hours Bill' [Nardinelli, 1990].

Secondly, there were the Tory humanitarians, among whom Lord Ashley was particularly active. They were concerned at the moral and religious deprivation of young workers and the ineffectiveness of existing protective legislation. To Ashley, it was the paternalistic duty of the ruling class to care for those who were unable to care for themselves. Children came into that category, and since he accepted that current industrial developments made it impossible to abolish juvenile employment, then it was the government's responsibility to make their labour more bearable.

A third group of reformers included 'romantics' like William Wordsworth, Robert Southey and William Cobbett, who looked back to a pre-industrial 'golden age', and blamed the Industrial Revolution for alienating workers from the land and forcing children to play a major part in the labour market. For Southey, the manufacturing system had spawned social evils (including child factory labour) commensurate with the wealth it had created. William Cobbett expressed contempt for the greed of industrialists and commented ironically on the 'surprising discovery' that 'our superiority over other nations, [was] owing to 300,000 little girls in Lancashire'. If these little girls were to work for two hours a day less than they currently did, the factory masters claimed 'it would occasion the ruin of the country; . . . it would enable other nations to compete with us, and thus make an end to our boasted wealth'. Industrialization, according to the 'romantics', had brought about a disastrous decline in children's working conditions and since it was impossible to return to the 'golden age' of rural England (whose evils they conveniently ignored), effective government regulation of juvenile labour was the only solution.

A fourth body of reformers came to the fore in the debates over amendments to the factory legislation which occurred in the 1840s. They included active supporters of *laissez-faire* principles, such as Thomas Babington Macaulay, who nonetheless argued for state regulation of child employment on economic and moral grounds. If youngsters were allowed to damage their health through excessive work, this would reduce their potential productivity in later life. In a foreshadowing of the eugenics debate at the end of the century, Macaulay warned that overworked boys would become 'a feeble and ignoble race of men, the parents of a more feeble and more ignoble progeny', and therefore a threat to the well-being of the nation. At the same time the lack of opportunity to receive a suitable education reinforced these adverse tendencies by stunting the intellect as well as the body. To Macaulay the restriction of child factory labour was a rational means of promoting investment in the country's future workforce.

To these groups identified by Nardinelli a fifth may be added – the government itself, especially from the 1830s, through its appointment of investigatory Select Committees and Royal Commissions to examine the child labour question, and subsequently through the reports of the inspectors whom it recruited to oversee the legislation enacted. It was Leonard Horner, one of the first factory inspectors, who in 1840 not only expressed hostility to the special exemptions accorded to the silk industry under the 1833 Factory Act but pinpointed a number of other weaknesses in the Act's application [Horner, 1840]. His suggestions for their rectification formed the basis of the new Factory Act passed in 1844. Again, about two decades later, it was concern expressed by one of Her Majesty's Inspectors of Schools over the serious educational deficiencies of children in industrial Staffordshire which began the process of extending factory legislation to pottery production in 1864 [Dupree, 1981]. Once the authority of the inspectors had been accepted in the 1830s they were able to accelerate bureaucratic involvement in the promotion of measures they deemed necessary. In this way, the 'protection of child labour was, to a large extent, taken out of the public domain, and discussed in detail within the factory inspectorate' [Cunningham, 1991].

Against this background of debate and of awareness of the inadequacy of earlier regulatory measures, the 1833 Factory

Act was passed. It excluded children under 9 from all textile mills, except those making silk, and between 9 and 11 (rising to 9 and 13 over an adjustment period of two and a half years) limited them to 8 hours a day, or 48 hours a week. Between 13 and 18 the working day of 'young persons' was restricted to 12 hours. In addition, the youngest category of workers had to attend school for two hours daily, and to produce a voucher proving this had been done, before they were allowed to continue working. Thus commenced the 'half-time' system of combined work and schooling which survived in textiles, albeit on a declining scale, until after the First World War. (Throughout that time, incidentally, it was widely supported by adult operatives, whose children were its principal recruits, and they firmly resisted efforts to phase it out [Clarke, 1985].) Finally, and most importantly, four inspectors were appointed in 1833 to ensure the Act's provisions were observed. Although their 'policing' role was at first resented by many mill owners and parents it was soon accepted as an integral part of the whole regulatory mechanism.

In promoting the legislation the government was responding to the findings of the 1833 Factory Inquiry Commission, which had recognized the need to protect the youngest and most vulnerable members of the labour force. Nevertheless, as Lord Althorp made clear when he introduced the Bill, the decision had not been taken lightly:

> He still entertained doubts of the propriety of the Legislature interfering between the master and servant, but he would admit that if children were placed in a situation in which they could not protect themselves, it was the duty of that House to afford protection to them.

On that basis not only was the 1833 Act passed but also subsequent legislation designed to safeguard children and young persons in a variety of spheres. Nevertheless the need for child labour continued to be accepted. Indeed, in their anxiety to secure a 10-hour working day for adult workers some operatives in the 1830s were prepared to accept a *lengthening* of the children's working day from 8 to 10 hours to achieve that end [Smelser, 1972]. Other commentators shared the view of James McCulloch when he noted gloomily in 1835 that if children were excluded from factories until they were 13, few would attend school. Instead most would be 'thrown loose upon the streets, to acquire a taste for idleness, and to be early initiated in the vicious practices prevalent amongst the dregs of the populace'.

A number of problems soon emerged following the implementation of the new Act. The first was the hostility of many factory owners not merely to the restrictions on hours imposed, or the duties involved in ensuring that young workers received schooling, but the fact that textiles had been singled out for special treatment. Samuel and William Greg were not alone in insisting that the health and morals of cotton workers were 'at least equal to those engaged in other occupations' [Ward, 1962]. Even 'benevolent' owners like the Gregs and the Ashworths, who already provided schooling for their workers, resented this selective demonstration of the coercive powers of the State. And for those without access to educational facilities, the provision of school places and teachers, as well as the checking up on the age and attendance of the workers and the regulation of their hours, represented an implicit 'tax' they were reluctant to pay. Some responded by recruiting cheap and inefficient teachers in order to obey the letter if not the spirit of the law. 'I have had to reject the school voucher of the fireman', complained Horner on one occasion, 'the children having been schooled in the coal-hole . . . It may be supposed that such a thing could only happen at the mill of some poor ignorant man, but that . . . was not the case. It occurred where a large capital must be embarked' [Ward, 1935]. Significantly there is no evidence of an above-average increase in literacy rates in the textile areas after 1835, when the legislation began to be applied [Nardinelli, 1980].

In order to continue running the mills for 12 or more hours a day, a number of factory owners adopted a complicated relay system for their child workers. It was a policy the inspectors themselves at first largely favoured. Some owners, however, especially of smaller mills, merely pretended to adopt relays whilst flouting the law and overworking the children. Proprietors of water-powered factories, where juvenile labour was still relatively important, were particularly hostile to the new restrictions.

A further difficulty was the attitude of parents, many of whom wanted their children to work even before they had reached the legal minimum age. At a time when there was still no compulsory registration of births (registration itself came only in 1837), compliant medical men were found who would testify that an underage child had the 'ordinary strength and appearance' of a 9 or 13 year old, this latter being the minimum age for a youngster to work longer hours as a 'young person'. In the larger towns there were also complaints that the regulations were frustrated by children changing jobs so frequently that the inspectors could not keep up with them [Cruickshank, 1981].

Another weakness was the reluctance of magistrates to impose penalties on those who broke the law, perhaps because of their friendship with an offending employer or because they believed that parents should be allowed to dispose of their children's labour as they thought fit. Even the Home Office, while instructing the inspectors to apply the rules more stringently, recognized the problem presented by JPs' unwillingness to convict [Ward, 1962].

A number of owners reacted to the new restrictions by dispensing with their youngest child workers rather than taking on the administrative responsibilities and expense which accompanied their recruitment. This temporarily reinforced the downward movement in the proportion of juveniles in the textile labour force which Nardinelli has identified as taking place before 1833. Only after 1850, when power looms were installed on an increasing scale in mills and children were employed, as half-timers, to tend them, did the proportion of youngsters in the textile workforce rise once more, to reach a peak in 1874 [Nardinelli, 1990].

In 1844 the passage of a new Factory Act reduced the minimum employment age to 8, but limited the working day of children between 8 and 13 to $6\frac{1}{2}$ or 7 hours, plus a half-day school session of 3 hours (reduced to $2\frac{1}{2}$ hours during the winter months for those attending in the afternoons). Horner argued that with these shorter hours, it would not harm a child of 8 to work in the mills 'and it would make up to many parents for the diminution of the wages by the reduction from eight hours' work, by enabling them to have another child employed. There would be a reduction in the payments to individuals, but the mass of parents would lose nothing' [Horner, 1840]. For the first time child workers in silk manufacture who were under the age of 11 were also covered by the Factory Regulations.

So, despite the problems of implementing the Act of 1833 and, to a lesser extent, that of 1844, positive benefits did accrue. Some masters, like Henry McConnel, the largest Manchester employer, observed the conditions of the legislation scrupulously from the start. In other cases, despite the inefficiency of certain factory schools, there were opportunities for many children to attend well-run establishments on factory premises or else ordinary elementary day schools in the neighbourhood. Employers, too, came to recognize the virtues of discipline and orderliness, and even of literacy and numeracy, which the schools could bestow and which

58

could be applied in the workplace. As a firm of Westmorland flax spinners reported approvingly, education had improved 'the conduct and habits of subordination of the factory hands generally' [Silver, 1977].

The 1833 and 1844 Factory Acts established the principles on which subsequent regulation was to be based. In 1847 and 1850 fresh legislation affected the working hours and conditions of young persons aged 13–18 and women, but did not directly influence the position of children. However, a new Act of 1853 did lay down that children were not to be employed before 6 a.m. or after 6 p.m. on weekdays, under normal circumstances, or after 2 p.m. on Saturdays. This followed a rule applied to young persons and women from 1850.

By the middle of the nineteenth century, therefore, the half-time system had been accepted not merely as an important strategy for combating excessive child labour but as a desirable educational innovation in its own right. The combination of school and industrial employment enabled poor children to gain both instruction and an income. As factory inspector Robert Baker declared in 1864, of the Potteries, the half-time arrangement was 'a godsend . . . , it being the only opportunity whereby the poor children can gain any education'. It was also claimed that the half-day school stint of three hours was the maximum amount of time any working-class child was capable of concentrating on academic work [Silver, 1977]. Some critics, admittedly, pointed out that half-timers who had spent the morning at work were so weary in the afternoon that they fell asleep at their desks. Others complained that when they went to ordinary elementary schools their intermittent attendance disrupted the timetable. There were also accusations that they undermined the moral standards of their full-time fellow pupils by their 'depraved' conduct. Nevertheless it was not until the 1870s that dissatisfaction with the half-time system became widespread, at a time when the increased provision of elementary schooling and the decline in child employment which accompanied it, highlighted the limitations of part-time education. It was at that stage that it began to be seen less as a 'rescue' mechanism than as a device for legitimizing the continuation of child labour.

The factory regulations of 1833 and 1844 had applied only to youngsters engaged in textile production. Over the years these principles were applied to other industries. At the same time they made acceptable the concept of State involvement in a variety of new social and educational spheres, ranging from smallpox vaccination offered by Poor Law guardians from the 1840s, to compulsory school attendance for all children, not merely those working in factories, in the 1870s and 1880s [Horn, 1990; Rose, 1991].

As regards the extension of factory legislation, that came only after the appointment of a Children's Employment Commission under pressure from Lord Shaftesbury, in 1861. This investigated the conditions of employment of children and young persons in trades not already covered by the law. As a result measures were introduced in 1864 and 1867 to cover such industries as pottery making, hosiery, lucifer match making, and various kinds of metalwork; lace manufacture had already been covered by a special Act of 1861. In addition, in a significant extension of control, regulation was applied under the 1867 Workshops Regulation Act to small units employing fewer than 50 people. That included the many children still engaged in cottage industries like straw-plaiting and gloving, but it presented particular problems of enforcement. Such small workplaces were extremely numerous and initially the task of regulation was given to local sanitary authorities rather than the factory inspectorate. Only when they proved unequal to the task did the factory inspectors assume responsibility in 1871. Even then, the locating, let alone the inspection, of backstreet workshops was a daunting task and the 1867 Workshops Act remained largely a dead letter.

Some manufacturers whose firms were covered by this fresh wave of legislation preferred to dispense with child labour altogether rather than accept the administrative responsibilities associated with it. The fact that night work was prohibited affected the attitude of some of the ironmasters, for example. One factory inspector claimed that as a consequence boys were 'practically expelled from the forges'. Certainly the number of boys under 13 employed in iron-making dropped from 2686 in 1867 to 62 in 1871, while in foundrywork there was a fall from 1014 to 137 over the same period. By contrast the number of males employed between 13 and 18 rose sharply [*Factories and Workshops, Reports*, 1872]. Some of the children who were excluded moved into industries which were still largely or entirely unregulated, such as agriculture (controlled only by the 1867 Agricultural Gangs Act), brickmaking (with small brickyards remaining unregulated until 1871), domestic service and street trading, or else, especially in the larger towns, they merely ran wild in the streets. A Liverpool factory inspector reported in the late 1860s that parents considered their children's earnings as half-timers to be so meagre that they preferred to keep them at home rather than have the trouble and expense of part-time school attendance. Hence the disillusioned comment of one critic in 1867: 'They are idling in the streets and wynds; tumbling about in the gutters; selling matches; running errands; working in tobacco shops, cared for by no man' [Rose, 1991]. It was to be the task of the Education Acts of the 1870s to deal with that situation.

The factory and workshop legislation was, therefore, patchy both in its scope and in its effectiveness even in 1867, when its main principles had been established. Some industries were regulated or partially regulated while others were still not covered. Different Acts also imposed different restrictions on employers and child workers, thereby creating confusion and dissatisfaction. For example, while half-timers in textile mills after 1844 were normally required to attend school for three hours daily, those covered by the 1845 Print Works Act were expected to attend for 30 days in each half-year. Under the 1867 Workshops Regulation Act the requirement was for 10 hours a week. Again, while children began working at the age of 8 in factories and workshops, 10 was the minimum for boys employed underground in the mining industry, and girls were excluded entirely from underground labour in mining. Not until 1874 was the minimum age for employment in textile mills raised to 10. Four years later this minimum was applied to other factories and workshops. The 1878 Factory Act also prohibited the use of child labour in certain branches of the white lead and other industries which were considered especially likely to damage their health. These included melting or annealing glass, dry grinding in the metal trade and the dipping of lucifer matches.

The main importance of the factory reform movement was, nevertheless, the way in which it gradually encouraged society to accept that the State had a responsibility to prescribe minimum conditions of existence for the most vulnerable sectors of the population. In that way it inspired the growth of collectivist social policies during the last quarter of the nineteenth century over a wide sphere.

(ii) Philanthropy and childhood deprivation

Rising public concern over the plight of factory children in the middle decades of the nineteenth century was matched by growing anxiety about the large numbers of destitute youngsters who wandered the streets of most major towns. In 1848 Lord Ashley referred to more than 30,000 'naked, filthy, roaming, lawless, and deserted children, in and about the metropolis', who earned a living as crossing sweepers, costermongers, errand boys and girls, and in similar casual occupations [Cunningham, 1991]. The investigations of Henry Mayhew confirmed the existence of numerous impoverished youngsters living on the fringes of society, and the stratagems they adopted in order to support themselves. One little girl, aged about 10, whose mother was dead and whose father was a drunken building worker, confessed to working on the streets when there was no food at home.

I goes to school when father has money. We lives very well then. I've kept myself for a whole week. I mind people's stalls, if they're away a bit . . . and I go errands. . . . I've got a halfpenny on a day, and a penny, and some bread perhaps, and I've lived on that. [Mayhew, 1968]

It was not just her miserable situation that struck Mayhew but the fact that neglected children such as she became 'habituated to street life', and were unable to adapt to any other. They remained fringe characters for the rest of their lives.

Other critics, concerned at the children's puny physique, anticipated the arguments of eugenists at the end of the century by warning of the danger posed for the future of the race. In 1842, Edwin Chadwick referred to the 'noxious physical agencies', which were producing a population with 'a perpetual tendency to moral as well as physical deterioration' [Floud and Wachter, 1982]. Surveys were conducted to compare the height of factory and non-factory children and to ascertain whether factory workers were particularly stunted. Beyond confirming the low stature of most working-class children, they reached no very firm conclusions.

Outside London, the larger towns and cities had their retinues of neglected, destitute and homeless youngsters who lived and worked on the streets, and found shelter under archways, in sheds, or in overcrowded lodging houses, when they had sufficient pennies to pay for a bed for the night. In Manchester in 1840, 3650 children were found by police to be sleeping rough, while in Sheffield a 'great number of vagrant children' were 'prowling' about [Cunningham, 1991].

As with the factory movement, the motives of reformers were mixed, but three main strands of thought can be identified – religion, self-interest, and humanitarianism. Linked to these was a belief in the efficacy of education in inculcating the values of hard work, morality and honesty and in countering the failures and deficiencies attributed to much of existing working-class life. Schooling was regarded as an 'insurance' to protect the respectable majority from the threat of political instability and crime.

Concern about destitute children became acute in the 1830s and 1840s partly as a result of the findings of the newly established statistical societies. They drew attention to the 'moral topography' of different districts and linked areas of social deprivation with juvenile delinquency. In 1850 Thomas Beames described the London rookeries as 'beds of pestilence' and nurseries of felons, 'where children were trained as criminals under professional thieves and became addicted to drink and debauchery' [May, 1973]. Contributing to the general unease was anxiety over the rapid growth of the urban population and of the rootlessness which characterized many slum dwellers.

The more sophisticated statistical methods used to analyse crime seemed to suggest that lawlessness was on the increase, especially among the young. The work of Evangelical missionaries revealed the general indifference towards religion and morality among large sections of the poor. In London, the City Mission, set up in 1835 to extend the knowledge of the gospel among these groups, soon became involved in educating destitute children in what were to become known as Ragged Schools. Significantly the Second Annual Report of the Ragged School Union (RSU), itself formed in 1844, defined its objectives as:

> to introduce among the most miserable and neglected outcasts in London, some knowledge of the commonest principles of morality and religion; to commence their recognition as immortal human creatures, before the Gaol Chaplain becomes their schoolmaster. [Clark, 1967]

By 1840 five schools had been established for 'children raggedly clothed', and four years later nineteen such institutions united to form the Ragged School Union, with Lord Ashley as president. Their importance lay in the fact that they catered for the poorest of the poor for whom no other kind of education was available. Their filthy condition as well as their inability to pay a school fee led to their exclusion from most ordinary elementary schools [*Education of Destitute Children, Select Committee*, 1861].

In organization and methods the Ragged Schools owed much to the inspiration of the earlier Sunday schools, which were now concentrating their efforts on 'respectable' children, and to the work of the City Mission. Average attendance in RSU day schools in London rose from 3480 in 1848 to 23,052 in 1870 and at the Sunday schools from 5843 to 29,778 over the same period. Night schools were also organized by the RSU for the often undisciplined youngsters who had to work during the day, and attendance at these rose from 3300 in 1848 to 9413 in 1860; it remained at around that figure for a further decade [Clark, 1969].

Self-interest was an important factor in encouraging charitable provision for destitute children, especially in the 1840s when political agitation associated with Chartism seemed to threaten the *status quo*. In 1850 a writer to the *Ragged School Union Magazine* praised the movement for keeping the populace

65

docile and making the idle industrious. Others claimed that petty theft had been reduced as a result of their efforts. This ambiguity of aim is emphasized by Elaine Hadley, who comments that it was not so much 'the rags and hungry eyes' of neglected children which encouraged philanthropic initiative as the image of 'jaunty clothing and a chop-house feast' obtained by delinquent youngsters through crime [Hadley, 1990]. The pejorative language often applied to street children, such as 'savages' or 'guttersnipes' was another manifestation of this anxiety about the challenge they offered to an ordered society. Such fears persuaded some of the more prosperous that certain forms of behaviour that might have been dismissed as youthful pranks were criminal acts. The belief that there was an upsurge in juvenile crime thus became a self-fulfilling prophecy [Walvin, 1982].

The third arm of the reform movement was humanitarian, arising out of concern for the misery experienced by many of the children. If they were to be rescued and rehabilitated, the corrupting influences of urban life must be countered, and it was in this connection that the Ragged Schools were particularly important. Not only did they provide a religiously-based education designed to civilize and reclaim those untouched by existing schools but they offered various schemes to modify the conduct of pupils. These included the setting up of refuges and night dormitories to provide shelter for the homeless, the promotion of temperance by forming branches of the Band of Hope, and the encouragement of thrift through the establishment of clothing clubs, savings banks, and similar agencies [Babler, 1986; Clark, 1967]. Treats and excursions were arranged and efforts made to raise moral standards throughout the surrounding area. The schools' promoters regarded them more as mission stations than as purely educational institutions, and unlike most other elementary schools, they laid great stress on the provision of free schooling. It was a policy criticized by some as rewarding the improvident. The Bristol penal reformer, Mary Carpenter, argued that such an attitude not only discouraged self-reliance but was unjust to the 'self-denying and industrious poor' because the 'profligate and careless' were given what they were 'obliged to toil for' [Clark, 1969]. However, the RSU responded by pointing out that many pupils were orphans or deserted children or the offspring of parents who lacked the means to pay school fees. A careful check was kept on parental circumstances to ensure that those who could afford to pay were excluded from the Ragged Schools. Other critics, like Henry Mayhew, condemned the schools as 'training institutions for criminals' because of the lawless conduct of some of those attending, and the way in which they terrorized their teachers – a charge which had some justification, even though most teachers were volunteers.

As part of its rehabilitation programme, the Union sought to find work for scholars. The migratory way of life of many of them made this difficult, but between 1853 and 1874 its local committees claimed to have helped over 34,000 children to find employment. Evidence suggests that for the boys the armed forces were a popular outlet, while for the girls the overwhelming choice was domestic service. To encourage settled habits, prizes were offered to youngsters who stayed in their post for at least a year [Babler, 1986; Clark, 1967].

Some pupils gained temporary work through the shoe-black brigades which were initiated in 1851. Their aim was to teach 'habits of industry' and by 1857 there were nine of them operating in London. Each member received a uniform and some shoe-cleaning equipment to enable him to earn a modest income and amass a few savings. These last were used for the boy's benefit when he quit the brigade. Although the RSU hailed the venture as offering healthy and remunerative employment, in practice it proved a blind alley occupation which did little to prepare the youngsters to find worthwhile work in later life.

Although London was a pioneer in setting up Ragged Schools, other towns and cities followed suit. In Hull, for example, a school was opened in 1849 to provide food, clothing and training for neglected and vagrant children. The boys learned shoemaking, joinery and tailoring, while the girls were taught housewifery skills. After 1868 the school ran a training ship to which delinquent boys were sent to learn practical seamen's skills as well as basic reading and writing [Cowan, 1984; Frostick, 1990]. By 1852, forty-one towns (including London) had Ragged Schools, 110 of them being in London and 70 in the provinces. Less than a decade later there were 64 Ragged Schools in Liverpool alone and it and Manchester had Unions along the lines of that in the capital. In 1861 Liverpool claimed an average attendance of 7678 children and Manchester of 3573 during the winter months [*Criminal and Destitute Juveniles, Select Committee*, 1852; *Education of Destitute Children, Select Committee*, 1861].

Some activists also undertook initiatives of their own. Thus Mary Carpenter, who pioneered Reformatory and Industrial schools for juvenile delinquents, gained valuable insights into childhood deprivation through her work at the Bristol Ragged School. And it was Dr Thomas Barnardo's encounters with homeless boys met through work at a Stepney Ragged School that encouraged him to provide the first of his refuges [Rose, 1987]. The proliferation of residential homes and refuges along lines similar to those of Dr Barnardo was, in part, a response to the powerful domestic ideology of the mid-Victorian period, because of the pseudo-familial atmosphere they sought to create.

It is important to remember, too, that these charitable endeavours often benefited the *providers* as well as the recipients, perhaps by satisfying a religious desire to 'do good' or by supplying an aim in life for those (especially women) whose existence lacked purpose. The sense of personal fulfilment which philanthropic action could bestow is exemplified by Lord Ashley's claim that he 'would rather be President of the Ragged School Union than have the command of armies or wield the destiny of empires' [Clark, 1969].

Emigration was seen by the RSU as a further means of providing for its pupils, by removing them permanently from the contaminating urban environment in which they had grown up. In this respect it was following the example of other societies working in the related fields of education and penal reform, such as the Philanthropic Society and the Children's Friend Society. This latter had begun life in 1830 as the Society for the Suppression of Juvenile Vagrancy, formed, in the words of its founder, 'for the purpose of clearing the streets of unemployed children, who swell the daily catalogue of juvenile offenders'. Although the Society changed its name in 1834, it continued to send children overseas, with approximately 1300 despatched by 1837, mostly to the southern part of Africa. Then came adverse publicity arising from critical letters written home by some boy emigrants and published in *The Times* in 1839. A year later the scheme ended [Bradlow, 1984; Hadley, 1990].

In 1848, however, Lord Ashley appealed for State help in sending Ragged School pupils to Australia, where the boys could find employment on sheep stations. As a first step funds were given to send 150 youngsters, but the government then refused to repeat the experiment. The RSU tried to continue the scheme on its own, but lack of cash and other difficulties led to its abandonment in the mid-1850s [Babler, 1986; Clark, 1967; Wagner, 1982].

Emigration appealed to many who worked with neglected children because it offered the prospects of employment in a healthy environment, where their labour was needed and where they were removed from the malign influences of

English city life. One enthusiast referred to it as a 'spring transplanting'. Elaine Hadley, less romantically, has labelled it 'a life sentence of transportation into the working class' for youngsters without regular employment in England [Hadley, 1990]. Yet despite several attempts to promote it as a solution to the problems of child destitution, juvenile emigration was not successful during this period. Its disadvantages outweighed its alleged benefits. Chief among these was the inability to guarantee the welfare of the children once they had been sent away. The similarity between emigration, offered as a reward for the 'deserving' child, and transportation, which until 1853 was a possible punishment for youngsters who had broken the law, was another difficulty, as was the ambivalent attitude of those who arranged the emigration. Most seemed uncertain whether their prime objective was to benefit the children or society at large, by removing unwanted, unemployed youngsters from areas where they posed a potential threat as criminals and troublemakers.

The same kind of ambiguity lay behind attempts to rehabilitate pauper children, following the passage of the 1834 Poor Law Amendment Act and its creation of a network of Poor Law Unions throughout the country. Here, again, the size of the problem gave a sense of urgency to the reformers, with almost half the workhouse population in 1838 consisting of juveniles, most of them without parents or close relatives [Pinchbeck and Hewitt, 1973; Crowther, 1982].

Prior to 1834 pauper children had been dealt with in a variety of ways. Some had been supported outside the workhouse through a system of income support paid to their families by means of Speenhamland-type arrangements. Others, who lived within the workhouse, might receive a modest degree of education and training along lines identified in the mid-1790s at Ashby-de-la-Zouch in Leicestershire:

the children are taught to read, to spin jersey, to do common house-work; spinning, knitting, sewing, working in the fields, &c. by which means they become early attached to industrious principles, and are thereby made truly useful and valuable servants. [Eden, 1966]

But all too easily this could lead to exploitation of the children involved, when they were farmed out to employers who had little regard for their welfare − as we saw in the case of some of the pauper apprentices. Elsewhere, as in parts of Kent and Lancashire, youngsters were sent out to the local elementary school to receive instruction if none was available in the workhouse itself. But, especially in rural areas, there were many parish poorhouses which gave no education to their child inmates, who were merely set to work on such tasks as were to hand. In Norfolk, for example, educational provision in most poorhouses has been described as non-existent prior to 1834, although in the boroughs they received instruction designed to inculcate the correct religious and moral attitudes. Thus at St James Workhouse in King's Lynn, each child learnt the Church Catechism and to read the Bible, so as to instil a sense of service and hard work. But teachers were lowly paid and largely untrained. In Norfolk it was common for the pauper child to be instructed by an adult inmate [Digby, 1978; Melling, 1964].

The 1834 Act was designed to end this unsystematic and variable approach. The main purpose of pauper education was seen as the separation of the children both from the workhouse itself and from other paupers. In this way youngsters would avoid the debilitating and demoralizing influence associated with adult pauperism and would learn to become self-dependent. One means of achieving this was for groups of Poor Law Unions to join together to set up district schools, capable of accommodating around 500 pupils. A broad education would be provided, including industrial training, and the children would avoid the stigma attached to work-house residence. However, partly for administrative reasons and partly because of friction with the Poor Law Commission and fears of the cost involved, little was done by the Unions to implement this scheme before the late 1840s. By 1849 only six school districts had been formed, three of them in London, although in Manchester and Liverpool separate Poor Law schools of industry had also been set up [Duke, 1976].

Unfortunately the scheme's disadvantages soon became clear. The large, barrack-like schools that resulted lacked the more intimate atmosphere which the better teachers were able to create in individual workhouse schools. There were allegations, too, of moral 'contamination' in the bigger institutions, with girls from the Liverpool school of industry drifting into prostitution. The pupils also lacked vitality and 'practical awareness', and the absence of normal domestic and family ties meant that females, in particular, were poorly prepared either for employment as servants or for the duties they would have to undertake as wives and mothers in later life. There was evidence, too, that children brought up in district schools were returning to the workhouses as adult paupers, although this was the one major trend the schools were supposed to avoid [Pinchbeck and Hewitt, 1973].

For these reasons, therefore, district schools remained few in number. Instead improvements were instituted within the workhouse schools which served a single Union, and that included the setting up of separate institutions away from the main workhouse premises in some cases. Here the children were segregated from the adults (including their own parents, if they were also workhouse inmates), so as to eradicate 'the germs of pauperism from the rising gener-ation', as James Kay put it in the late 1830s [Digby, 1978]. That was something which the Poor Law system of class-ifying inmates by age and sex in any case facilitated. Rudimentary industrial training was combined with academic lessons to prepare them for a life of independent toil, but like many other organizations catering for the destitute, the main underlying objectives continued to be social control and work discipline. 'Imparting good education to the poorest classes is equivalent to an insurance on our property', declared a Poor Law Inspector. 'No money seems to return so good an interest as that which is laid out in securing the morals of the labouring classes' [Duke, 1976].

As with emigration, it was unclear whether Poor Law education was designed to improve the lives and prospects of the pupils or to suppress crime and political discontent. In any event, life for most inmates of Poor Law institutions was depressingly dreary. Teaching was unimaginative and except for occasional outings there was no escape from the drudging daily routine. The generally poor physical condition of many of the inmates, which arose from the poverty in which they had been born and bred, and the large numbers congregating together in the bigger schools, led to outbreaks of epidemic disease, especially contagious ophthalmia and skin complaints [Pinchbeck and Hewitt, 1973]. Not until the 1880s could the youngsters enjoy such 'luxuries' as balls or swings within establishments which were, in essence, concerned with depauperization and deterrence. It was from the 1870s, too, that experiments began in boarding out orphaned children from the workhouse with foster parents and in setting up cottage homes designed to accommodate small groups of children, and to give something of a family atmosphere [Pinchbeck and Hewitt, 1973].

From the mid-1850s Poor Law Unions were also empowered to pay the school fees of pauper children resident outside the workhouses whose parents were in receipt of outdoor relief. In practice, on grounds of cost few chose to do so before the 1870s. Most such youngsters were thus prevented from obtaining an education unless they were catered for by charity, including the Ragged Schools.

In the case of pauper education it was the State rather than philanthropy which played the decisive role. In coping with children who had broken the law or seemed in danger of doing so, the State and charitable endeavour worked in tandem.

During the early nineteenth century juvenile criminals were punished in much the same way as adults. The only differences were that up to the age of 7, children were deemed incapable of criminal intent and from 7 to 14 they were presumed innocent unless the prosecution proved their ability to discern between good and evil. Thereafter they were fully responsible [May, 1973]. Young offenders were tried with the full ceremonial of the law and if found guilty were liable to capital punishment, transportation or imprisonment, including solitary confinement. They had no legal right to be treated differently from adults, although compassion might be exercised on their behalf because of their youth. Thus of 103 children under 14 given capital sentences at the Old Bailey between 1801 and 1836, all were commuted to transportation or imprisonment [May, 1973; Bradlow, 1984]. Nevertheless as early as 1818 a Select Committee complained of the 'contamination' which resulted from the free association of prisoners in many gaols, with 'children of the tenderest age . . . confined . . . with prisoners of more mature age and more confirmed habits of crime'. Recommital statistics confirmed that juveniles were not deterred by their confinement. 'They become trained to prison life', concluded the Select Committee on Prison Discipline in 1850. For this reason, many witnesses to official inquiries into juvenile crime favoured whipping as a legal punishment. They argued it was better to beat a child than to send it to prison for a relatively minor transgression and thereby brand it for life as a criminal [Walvin, 1982].

At the same time it was recognized that for some destitute children gaol might be a welcome alternative to life on the

74

streets. Prison clothing was thicker than their own rags and the meals they were given were superior to the food they could buy, beg or pilfer for themselves [Tobias, 1967]. In addition, under the 1823 Gaols Act provision was to be made for prisoners to be taught to read and write. The effectiveness of this varied considerably. In a number of cases, as at Exeter Borough Prison, responsibility for instruction seems to have been handed over to the chaplain [Forsythe, 1983]. Elsewhere, including Derby and Leicester, a schoolmaster had been specially appointed by 1826, while at Maidstone the duty of teaching juvenile prisoners to read devolved on one of the turnkeys. But there were also prisons which followed the example of Norwich House of Correction in declaring firmly: 'No convenience can be made for a School. The Prisoners are supplied with . . . Books.' These were seemingly of little benefit if they were unable to read!

As mid-century social investigations revealed the scale of childhood deprivation and suggested its link with juvenile crime, so greater emphasis was placed on the need for a programme of reform. As a first step child prisoners were to be separated from adults, and it was in this context that Parkhurst prison was opened in 1838 as the first juvenile gaol. Yet, despite its avowed intention of reforming offenders, deterrence and harsh treatment became its chief characteristics. Nothing was to be done to 'weaken the terror of the law or . . . lessen in the minds of the juvenile population at large . . . the dread of being committed to prison' [Pinchbeck and Hewitt, 1973]. For this reason Parkhurst failed to meet Mary Carpenter's requirement that 'children should not be dealt with as men but as children'. Its failure to overcome initial adverse publicity led to the closure of its juvenile section in 1864.

A more positive attempt to deal with juvenile delinquency came in the 1850s, shortly after the ending of transportation, with the setting up of Reformatory and Industrial schools.

These were hybrid institutions, founded and partly financed by voluntary effort but given legislative sanction in 1854 and 1857 respectively, and subject to government inspection. Reformatories were intended for those under 16 who had committed crimes punishable with imprisonment, while Industrial schools catered for children under 14 who had committed less serious offences or were living in conditions likely to lead to their becoming criminals. This might be as a result of parental neglect, and no parent was to be allowed to bring up a child so as to 'almost secure his becoming a criminal' [May, 1973; Stack, 1982]. Unfortunately the vocational training they provided to rehabilitate their inmates had the unintentional side-effect of associating schools for industrial, trade and technical training with deviance, criminality and punishment. This helped to make England resistant to technical and trade schools for non-criminal children later on − a point frequently made in the 1890s and 1900s.

Contemporaries attributed the sharp drop in juvenile crime which followed these initiatives to the effects of the new schools. The fact that children were confined in Reformatories for at least two years, compared with the prison sentences of one or three months which had been common under the old regime, was felt to give time for reform and a severing of undesirable connections. Also significant was the fact that youngsters lost some of their skills, especially as pickpockets, through being confined. In 1864, Mary Carpenter claimed that the work habits the Reformatory inmates acquired made employers eager to recruit them. But even when a boy's conduct was not improved by sending him to a Reformatory, the experiment was considered worthwhile if it removed from society the more experienced child criminals who were likely to corrupt other youngsters. In this way, it was hoped, the ranks of juvenile delinquents would be thinned and the vicious circle which perpetuated the existence of the criminal classes broken. By 1872 there were 55

Reformatories in operation, including three training ships, and they accommodated 3522 male offenders and 846 females. In addition, there were 71 Industrial schools, catering for 4418 boys and 1380 girls [*Population Census*, 1873].

Although there were complaints that discipline in the schools was oversevere, that the education provided was of poor quality, and that the buildings, food and clothing were unsatisfactory, this should not obscure their revolutionary role with regard to the position of the deprived child in society. They gave to juvenile delinquents a new legal status and acknowledged their potential for growth and reform, in contrast to the retributive punishment administered to hardened adult criminals. The schools were intended to act as 'moral hospitals', or as the commander of the Liverpool-based Reformatory ship *Akbar* put it: 'the first great change which has to be affected [sic] . . . when they are received on board in their vagrant state is to make them "boys". They are . . . too knowing, too sharp when they come on board, too much up in the ways of the world' [May, 1973].

However, not all agreed with this approach and since the 1854 Reformatory legislation was permissive, some magistrates continued to take the view that lawless youngsters needed the sharp lesson of a prison sentence rather than the reformist approach of the schools. In other cases, children were sent to Reformatories rather than Industrial Schools even when they had committed no crime, a policy castigated by the Inspector of Reformatory and Industrial Schools as likely to injure them through association with lads much further advanced in crime than themselves [*Reformatory and Industrial Schools*, 1871].

As with many aspects of the treatment of the deprived child, society was unable to decide whether its best interests were served by punishment and deterrence or by reform and rehabilitation. For many mid-Victorians there was only a flimsy partition between the poor but honest child and the criminal [Hadley, 1990]. Nonetheless, while the scale of progress made should not be overestimated, by the 1850s and 1860s there was a greater understanding of the special problems of poor children and an appreciation, through the Industrial School system, that the State had a right to act *in loco parentis* where parents were failing to provide for the physical, mental and moral welfare of their offspring. Similar concern to protect the welfare of children working in a growing range of industries was also displayed through the passage of more stringent factory legislation from the 1830s onwards, culminating in the Factory and Workshop Acts of 1867. In this fashion the way was prepared for later measures concerned with child protection. The special position of juveniles was accepted and in that respect there was a favourable contrast with the harsh and hostile approach adopted towards deprived and delinquent youngsters at the beginning of the century. As a mid-Victorian calm settled on the country, writes Cunningham, 'it became possible to picture the children in a more relaxed and tolerant way. There was sometimes pity for these children, there was sometimes annoyance . . . but there was no longer any suggestion . . . that the future of the country was threatened by their existence' [Cunningham, 1991].

4 Work and Welfare: 1868–1880s

Despite earlier efforts by the religious denominations and other voluntary bodies to provide a network of elementary schools for working-class children, there was at the end of the 1860s a substantial minority of youngsters who were still receiving little or no education [Hurt, 1979]. Sometimes, especially in remote rural areas or in the overcrowded slums of the major cities, this was because of a shortage of school places for them. Indeed, there is evidence that an already unsatisfactory situation may even have worsened in some larger towns during the 1850s and 1860s. A comparison of statistics in the 1851 Education Census and the 1869 governmental inquiry into day school provision in Birmingham, Leeds, Liverpool and Manchester indicates the pressures faced in keeping up with population expansion. Although in both Manchester and Birmingham this seems to have been achieved, in Leeds and Liverpool it was not. Thus in Leeds, while population rose by around 50 per cent over the period, pupils on the books of day schools increased by only about 30 per cent; for Liverpool, the corresponding figures were around 30 per cent and almost 20 per cent. Furthermore, the fact that nearly a third of the pupils in Leeds and Liverpool in 1869 were on the rolls of private and other non-inspected schools, which might offer a very poor quality of instruction, underlines the difficulty [*Education: Reports*, 1870].

In other cases the failure of children to attend school was due to parental apathy or poverty. In 1864 a Factory

Inspector claimed sourly that as long as parents could 'both get their children out of the way and make money by it too, instead of paying for schooling, . . . they will do it'. For the cost of a child's education was not merely the weekly fee of 1d. or 2d. paid to the school but the loss of a wage of perhaps 9d. to 1s. 6d. a week, which many were unwilling to forego. Not until 1891 were fees abolished in most elementary schools.

But most alarming to many contemporaries was the discovery that large numbers of school-age children were neither being educated nor working; in respect of Liverpool, Birmingham and Manchester these might amount to 25 to 30 per cent of the total, according to the estimate of George Melly MP, in 1869 [*Hansard*, 1868–9]. The situation was aggravated in certain districts by the effects of the Factory and Workshop Acts of 1864 and 1867 since these had encouraged some employers to dispense with young workers. They were then added to the army of youngsters wandering the streets or taking casual work as costermongers and errand boys (see Chapter 3[i]).

It was to remedy this situation, with many non-attenders allegedly in danger of drifting into 'habits of vagrancy, mendicancy, and crime', as Melly put it, that in 1870 W. E. Forster introduced the Elementary Education Bill. It was designed to fill the gaps in the existing voluntary system and to provide every child with a school place in a building of reasonable quality and with a qualified head teacher. Forster argued that one of the Bill's prime purposes was to remove ignorance 'which we are all aware is pregnant with crime and misery, with misfortune to individuals and danger to the community'. But there was a knowledge, too, that Britain's economic future depended upon the production of a skilled and well-educated labour force and an awareness that foreign rivals were taking action where she was failing:

It is of no use trying to give technical teaching to our artisans without elementary education . . . and if we are to hold our position among . . . the nations of the world we must make up the smallness of our numbers by increasing the intellectual force of the individual. [*Hansard*, 1870]

In districts where the voluntary schools were unable to cater for all the children living within their area the deficiency was to be met by the setting up of rate-aided school boards, elected from the ratepayers. They were empowered not only to build schools but to introduce compulsory school attendance for children between the ages of 5 and 10 and thereafter to 12 or 13, according to local by-laws, unless youngsters could pass a leaving examination or gain exemption in some other way. For the first time the principle of compulsion – albeit at this stage a 'permissive' compulsion – was extended beyond children in factories and workshops, Poor Law institutions, Reformatories and Industrial Schools to the wider juvenile population. In 1876 and 1880 these provisions were extended until in the latter year compulsory schooling was unequivocally applied to all youngsters within the relevant age range.

Initially, despite the employment of attendance officers, enforcement of the regulations proved difficult. James Reeves, who worked in London, remembered that one of his early duties was to visit an old-established market in Bethnal Green which was attended by boys and girls seeking hire on two days a week. 'The names and addresses of the children were taken, and the parents influenced to send them to school' [Reeves, 1913]. There were, however, three problems to be faced in achieving this end.

The first, especially in large cities like London, was a need to increase the number of school places to accommodate the additional pupils. In London, a quarter of a million places had to be supplied and even at the end of the century many temporary buildings were still in use [Horn, 1989]. In Bradford the imposition of compulsory by-laws was delayed until 1872, when sufficient temporary accommodation had been acquired to make it a realistic proposition. Secondly, parents resented any interference with their right to dispose of their children's time and labour as they thought fit. And the fact that, except in cases of great need, school fees had to be paid, added to their dissatisfaction. Where children arrived at school without their pence they might be excluded by the teacher and if this proved a persistent difficulty, parents could be prosecuted. Thirdly, and associated with the latter point, there was the perhaps understandable reluctance of magistrates to impose penalties in attendance by-law cases if they thought this would mean hardship for the parents [Rubinstein, 1969]. Hence backsliders were often not fined even when the regulations were blatantly ignored. In 1884, for example, the London school board unsuccessfully prosecuted the father of a 12-year-old girl who was working as a nursemaid even though she had not reached the educational standard which permitted early exemption from school. The case went to appeal but the judge upheld the original verdict, claiming that the girl had been 'discharging the honourable duty of helping her parents, and . . . before I held that these facts did not afford a reasonable excuse for her non-attendance . . . , I should require to see the very plainest words to the contrary in the [Education] Act' [Rubinstein, 1969].

Nevertheless, despite these difficulties large numbers of deprived children were brought into the elementary school system for the first time. Their presence created disciplinary problems for teachers, especially in view of the large size of many classes. One of H.M. Inspectors of Schools working in Cumberland, Westmorland and Lancashire welcomed the 'large influx of rough and ragged children . . . in . . . bare feet and tattered clothes'; 'one cannot but hail with inward rejoicing the first unmistakable signs of the great moral good which the recent Act is calculated to do for the poor neglected children, that swarm about the lanes and alleys' [Hurt, 1979]. He also recognized the difficulty posed for teachers by 'the reluctant presence ... of even a few ... embryo Artful Dodgers' [Horn, 1989]. As J. S. Hurt graphically puts it, one of the main aims of the 1870 Act had been 'to bring the social and the educational outcasts of the nation into the schools'.

The fulfilment of this objective brought with it a gradual raising of literacy and numeracy standards among the most deprived groups in society. But it had a number of largely unforeseen welfare implications as well. Foremost among these was an appreciation of the large amount of malnourishment among the nation's children and a realization that it was impossible for pupils to benefit from the education provided if they were hungry. This kind of 'value for money' argument proved particularly persuasive among those who, in principle, supported a *laissez-faire* approach. Teachers like the headmistress of Orange Street Girls' School in Southwark, London, began to provide meals of bread, tea, coffee and warm milk for some pupils, and out of initiatives of this kind there developed a number of school breakfast and dinner societies designed to supply free or cheap meals. In London, there were six major organizations in operation at the end of the 1880s, as well as a number of minor ones. In the year up to March 1889 they provided school board pupils alone with 7943 free breakfasts, 26,585 free dinners, and a further 13,900 meals at costs ranging between a farthing and a penny each. But it was recognized that for the poorest children even these modest charges were too high. Only free meals were of use to them [*School Board for London, 1889*]. Furthermore, despite this formidable charitable effort, of the estimated 12.8 per cent of pupils in the capital's board schools who were habitually short of food at the end of the 1880s, less than half were being fed by these voluntary schemes. In Manchester, Birmingham and Liverpool similar voluntary arrangements were also in operation but, again, the scale of need outstripped the philanthropic initiatives taken. The Birmingham Schools Cheap Dinner Society, formed in October 1884, for example, rapidly discovered that many scholars were so poor that they 'could no more find a halfpenny for a dinner than they could find a half-sovereign' [Hurt, 1979].

Also highlighted by attendance at school was the high level of dirt and sickness among the most deprived children. Epidemic diseases were constantly mentioned in school log books for all classes of elementary pupils, but the problem was most severe among the slum dwellers. 'The provision of a bath to wash the Boys' persons, and an oven to bake their clothes, is extremely desirable', commented one Inspector after a visit to Orange Street Boys' School in 1877; 'and the wretched state of many homes in this locality calls loudly for the application of the Artisans' Dwelling Act.' Twelve years later, despite improvements, difficulties remained, with some of the children 'still sadly dirty. Years ago I recommended that means should be found for washing their persons and freeing their clothes from vermin. In a similar school the Birmingham School Board is setting up a bath – a most beneficial measure not yet tried in London.' Likewise at Nichol Street Boys' School, also in London, the Inspector suggested that because many of the boys were 'so ragged . . . some instruction in mending their clothes would be very useful to them'.

Although critics like the Charity Organization Society could argue that it was the improvidence of working-class families rather than low income which was responsible for youngsters' poverty and ill-health, most appreciated that the need was genuine. By 1878 there were 50 philanthropic societies catering for children in London alone. But beyond

84

that broad charitable framework, public opinion was still reluctant to stray. Despite the growth of collectivist sentiment, fear of infringing parental rights and undermining the self-dependence of the working-class family prevented State intervention during this period to provide school meals and medical examinations for the elementary schoolchild. Even intervention to protect the health and well-being of infants was opposed by many. 'I would far rather see . . . a higher rate of infant mortality prevailing than has ever yet been proved . . . than intrude one iota farther on the sanctity of the domestic hearth and the decent seclusion of private life', declared Whately Cooke Taylor in 1874 [Pinchbeck and Hewitt, 1973]. At that time about one in six of all babies born in England was dying before its first birthday, and even modest measures like the Infant Life Protection Act, 1872, designed to protect infants put out to paid nurses, proved a virtual dead letter from its earliest days [Rose, 1986].

A more encouraging effect of the 1870 Elementary Education Act was the boost it gave to the schooling of the handicapped child. Under the terms of the Act provision had to be made for all children, and although the handicapped were not specifically mentioned, neither were they excluded. Reactions varied but as early as 1872 the London school board was discussing the possible supply of places to blind and deaf children. Two years later the first class for the deaf was established and in 1875 provision was made for the blind also [*Final Report of London School Board*, 1904; Pritchard, 1963]. Hitherto education of the handicapped had depended on voluntary effort and had been mainly in residential institutions. Although the scale of the London initiative remained small for many years, it paved the way for wider reforms. Sheffield, for example, opened a class for the deaf in 1879 and in the following decade, Leeds, Nottingham, Bradford and a number of other towns followed suit. In Bradford the first step was taken after representations from the local Deaf and Dumb Institution, which agreed to contribute towards the salary of the teacher. Similarly Sunderland and Bradford school boards arranged for blind children to be taught in centres attached to certain of the ordinary elementary schools. For children with learning difficulties special Standard O classes were also formed, but where no such provision was made, groups of these children could be found clogging up the lower levels of other classes [Pritchard, 1963]. Unlike deafness and blindness, which were obvious physical handicaps, mental retardation was less conspicuous and thus easier to ignore. Not until the 1890s was a major attempt made to cater for the special needs of the mentally handicapped child [Hurt, 1988].

After 1870 the poverty and hardship of family life among the urban poor were revealed through school records and through the reports of teachers on their pupils. But the growing provision of full-time education in government-inspected schools also encouraged renewed debate over the merits of the half-time system organized under the Factory Acts. Whereas in the 1830s and 1840s this had often been presented as a 'rescue' agency designed to give young workers a modicum of schooling and to limit the length of their working day, by the 1870s and 1880s perceptions were changing. Already in 1874 and 1878 fresh legislation had raised the minimum working age for half-timers from 8 to 10 but there were still enthusiasts like Karl Marx who saw a positive educational and economic benefit in the blending of work and schooling. In 1875 Marx, in a well-known quotation, maintained that to prohibit child labour would not only be incompatible with 'the existence of large-scale industry' but would be reactionary, 'since, with a strict regulation of the working time . . . and other safety measures . . . an early combination of productive labour with education is one of the most potent means for the transformation of present day society' [Silver, 1977]. By combining education, physical

86

exercise and manual labour, Marx argued, not only would industrial efficiency be increased but a 'fully developed human being' would be produced.

The half-time system also retained its support among adult workers in its Lancashire and West Riding of Yorkshire heartlands, largely, it was claimed, because of the selfish desire of parents to benefit from their children's labour and because, as they themselves had worked as half-timers, they saw no harm in the arrangement.

However, many outsiders who witnessed half-time working at first hand rather than, like Marx, from a distance only, were less sanguine. By the 1880s there was a growing belief that it was merely reducing the educational opportunities of the children involved and supplying employers with cheap labour without giving the youngesters concerned any worthwhile benefit. In 1891 A. J. Mundella, a former Vice-President of the Education Department, condemned as 'one of the most preposterous fallacies ever trotted out by an interested class to hoodwink the community' the argument that the half-time combination of school and 'technical education' sharpened the children's wits [Silver, 1977]. Significantly with improved technology and changing attitudes the proportion of half-timers employed in textile factories moved steadily down from 12.5 per cent of the total workforce in 1874 to 8.9 per cent in 1885 and 7.8 per cent in 1890 [Nardinelli, 1990].

Finally, the growing emphasis on the welfare of the individual child led to a greater willingness to protect juveniles against ill-treatment and exploitation by parents as well as by other adults. The increasing concern about the employment of youngsters out of school hours as street vendors, errand boys and girls, domestic workers and the like was reflected in initiatives taken in the 1880s by municipalities like Manchester, Sheffield, Birmingham, Liverpool and Newcastle-on-Tyne in seeking to ban very young children from trading on the streets and prohibiting older ones from working after dark [Keeling, 1914]. This process was assisted by the setting up in Liverpool of the first English Society for the Prevention of Cruelty to Children in 1883. It was based upon a New York model and was followed in July 1884 by a similar body in London. Both organizations had as their prime objective the protection of children against physical ill-treatment but their interest also extended to what the London Society called 'Child Slaves'. These were youngsters sent out to beg or hawk on the streets until late at night [*London Society PCC*, 1887].

Five years later, under the leadership of the London organization, the National Society for the Prevention of Cruelty to Children was set up. The new organization controlled thirty-two provincial aid committees and was in the process of forming seven more. Shortly after, largely as a result of lobbying by the London members, the 1889 Prevention of Cruelty to Children Act was passed. It not only laid down penalties for the ill-treatment and neglect of children but prohibited the employment of any boy aged 10–14 or girl aged 10–16 in singing or performing for profit, or offering goods for sale, on the streets or on licensed premises (except those licensed for public amusement) between 10 p.m. and 5 a.m. [Rose, 1991; Behlmer, 1982]. Children under 10 were prohibited from carrying out these activities at any time and fines or imprisonment could be imposed on those causing youngsters to break the law. In cases involving parental mistreatment, children could be removed to a place of safety pending the trial of the parent and if there were a conviction, could then be entrusted to a relative or other 'fit person' (which included charitable institutions) for safety.

Unfortunately, as with much legislation involving children, enforcement proved difficult until boosted by further measures in the 1890s and beyond. For all its weaknesses, however, the 1889 Act was England's first attempt to deal comprehensively with the domestic relationship between parents and children. 'Limitations on parental power over their offspring . . . were now made explicit in a single statute', declares George Behlmer [1982]. The State had demonstrated a readiness to intervene within the hitherto sacred confines of the home by seeking to protect children against cruelty and abuse by members of their own family.

Concern for the sexual welfare of young girls had been one of the reasons behind the restrictions imposed on their trading in the streets at night by the 1889 Prevention of Cruelty to Children Act. An even more direct expression of anxiety over the issue of juvenile prostitution was reflected in efforts to raise the age of consent. Already in 1871 the Royal Commission on the Working of the Contagious Diseases Acts had drawn attention to the widespread 'traffic in children for infamous purposes . . . in London and other large towns. We think that a child of twelve can hardly be deemed capable of giving consent and should not have the power of yielding up her person. We therefore recommend the absolute protection of female children to the age of fourteen, making the age of consent to commence at fourteen instead of twelve as under the existing law' [Stafford, 1964]. However, when a Private Member's Bill sought to carry this into effect four years later it was rejected by the House of Lords, which refused to raise the age even to 13. Only after the Bill had returned to the Commons and it had been pointed out that the Factory Acts and the 1870 Education Act had concurred in making 13 the age at which childhood should end, did the Upper House relent. The age of 13 thus became the age of consent also. Not until a decade later, and following another bitter struggle, did the Criminal Law Amendment Act, 1885, raise that minimum age to 16.

Three years before, a Select Committee had claimed that juvenile prostitution, 'from an almost incredibly early age' was on the increase, especially in London. Various reasons were given for this, including 'a vicious demand for young girls', particularly in the West End of London, the effects of overcrowding in the home, a lack of parental moral influence, and a desire on the part of the girls to obtain the money and clothes which prostitution could bring. The 1885 Act was designed to make this illegal for youngsters under 16.

By the 1880s, therefore, interest in the welfare of children had spread beyond the earlier preoccupation with working hours, school provision and penal reform to cover a wide range of issues. In bringing about this change the 1870 Elementary Education Act and the collectivist spirit it represented had played an important role. Admittedly, as E. G. West pointed out long ago, most children were attending school for some part of their lives even before the Act was passed [West, 1975]. It was the poor and deprived youngsters who benefited from what Nigel Middleton has labelled this new 'legally enforced activity lasting several hours'. He charts the resultant change of attitude as exemplified in the legal actions taken:

> Before the 1870 Act there had been some fragmentary mention of children in the Statute Books. The Lord High Chancellor had as one of his traditional duties that of acting as guardian to all infants; in fact he only acted when property was involved, and then only rarely. The mass of children had been ignored, except when some high-minded person had managed to stir the public conscience. . . . Once children had been called to the attention of the country by assembling them in schools, measures to improve their depressed state followed in profusion. [Middleton, 1970]

These included no less than twenty Acts in the educational sphere alone between 1870 and 1900, as well as a wide range of other legislation. 'This ... interest in children's welfare even affected the stubborn problem of child prostitution' [Middleton, 1970].

As we have seen, many of the initial reforms were ineffective and required strengthening through subsequent action. But they had begun a process whereby the position of the child had changed from that of being one of the least considered members of society to one receiving a safer passage through the vulnerable years of immaturity and some opportunity to prepare for the responsibilities of adult life.

Conclusion: The Working-class Child in the 1880s

Partly as a result of the passage of labour and education legislation and partly through changing economic and social conditions, the century after 1780 saw a progressive lengthening of childhood as a stage in life. In the 1840s, 8 became established as the minimum age for half-time employment in textile mills and by the end of the 1860s that had been extended to a number of other important manufacturing processes as well as to cottage industries and public agricultural gangs. During the 1870s this minimum was raised to 10, while 13 was accepted as the age at which childhood officially ended. In addition, certain jobs were identified as unsuitable for children to carry out, and recognition was given to the fact that such youngsters lacked the intellectual and physical powers of adults when it came to bargaining over employment conditions. Children were accepted as 'special' cases who could be protected by legislation without infringing current *laissez-faire* philosophy.

In the late eighteenth century the childhood of the lower orders had been regarded largely as a time of preparation for the world of work. By the later nineteenth century it was being seen as a period in life which had its own 'dynamics and culture', as Cunningham puts it [Cunningham, 1991]. This concept was applied to all social classes and geographical regions. Play and pleasure were accepted as important for the children of the poor as well as for those from more prosperous homes. And as the size of families began to decline from the 1860s and 1870s, so the value of the individual child increased [Wrigley and Schofield, 1981].

Within the family and in the workplace, discipline became less severe than it had been at the beginning of the nineteenth century, and corporal punishment was less readily applied. The passage of legislation in 1889 designed to protect children against ill-treatment by parents as well as other adults was a symbol of the changing approach. Anti-cruelty measures were concerned to uphold children's rights and to enforce minimal parental duties. Nevertheless many youngsters continued to be subject to 'repressive paternalism' [Hendrick, 1992]. The regulation of children's behaviour, in the interests of teaching them to distinguish between right and wrong and of maintaining order within the home, continued to be a fundamental part of most parents' relationships with their offspring. Similarly, although the special position of young delinquents was recognized with the establishment of Reformatory and Industrial Schools in the 1850s, discipline remained severe in response to middle-class fears about the contaminating effect of juvenile crime and depravity.

Finally, the half-time system, once hailed as a means of protecting working children against excessive hours and exploitation, in the 1880s came to be seen as a means of perpetuating premature labour and of reducing the educational opportunities of those involved. Anxiety was growing, too, about the large number of young casual workers, often employed for long periods out of school hours as errand boys and girls, shop assistants, street traders and domestic workers of many kinds. Linked to this, especially following the advent of compulsory education, was an increasing awareness of the poor health of many youngsters from urban slums.

These fears were underlined by various social surveys undertaken in the 1880s and 1890s, notably by Charles

Booth in London and Seebohm Rowntree in York. Their findings were to reinforce the worries of imperialists over the rise of foreign commercial and military competition, especially from Germany, and the danger this posed for Britain's position as a world power. In this context concern to improve not only educational standards but the physical welfare of children seemed a sensible precaution, since they were to be the future protectors of the Empire. It would be impossible for the nation to defend itself properly if it had to rely on the 'rickety shoulders' of so many existing elementary pupils, born and bred in the unhealthy atmosphere of big cities like London, Manchester, Birmingham and Liverpool. In addition, the eugenists, with their preoccupations over national degeneracy, stressed the need for the future parents of the race to be fit and strong. For girls this led to a greater emphasis within the school curriculum on domestic subjects like sewing and cookery, designed to make them better wives and mothers.

These, then, were the issues which were to lend a sense of urgency to the campaign for 'national efficiency' from its infancy in the 1880s to its full development in the early twentieth century [Hendrick, 1990; Searle, 1976]. As the campaign gathered momentum it was to exert a growing influence on society's attitudes towards the working-class child.

Appendices

Appendix 1 Main Occupations of Children Aged 5–9 and 10–14 in 1851 and 1871

		Children aged 5–9			
Boys	1851	1871	Girls	1851	1871
Ag. labour	5,463	3,212	Straw plait	2,746	1,589
Messenger	2,158	255	Lace	2,590	626
Cotton man.	2,072	2,589	Cotton man.	1,477	2,182
Worsted	1,654	1,576	Worsted	1,271	1,914
Straw, &c work	1,422	462	Woollen man.	814	261
Coalmining	1,209	219	Hosiery	762	140
Total in age group	1,050,228	1,350,819	*Total in age group*	1,042,131	1,355,707
Total in age group at work	21,483	11,511	*Total in age group at work*	14,939	9,949
% at work	*2.0*	*0.9*	*% at work*	*1.4*	*0.7*

		Children aged 10–14			
Boys	1851	1871	Girls	1851	1871
Ag. labour	73,054	71,417	Domestic service (general)	50,065	89,699
Messenger	38,130	36,585	Cotton man.	29,038	43,150
Farm servt.	25,667	21,942	Worsted	10,586	12,876
Cotton man.	25,613	31,134	Silk	10,533	7,344
Coalmining	23,038	27,502			
Labourer (gen.)	13,478	21,177	Farm service	10,085	1,984
Shoemaker	9,700	6,525	Lace	8,628	5,240

Children aged 10–14

Boys	1851	1871	Girls	1851	1871
			Woollen man.	7,333	7,304
Total in age group	963,995	1,220,770	Total in age group	949,362	1,203,469
Total in age group at work	352,599	392,241	Total in age group at work	188,977	246,829
% at work	36.6	32.1	% at work	19.9	20.5

Source: 1851 and 1871 Census Reports. Order of ranking based on *1851 Census*.

NB: The figures are likely to be *underestimates* in that many part-time, casual and seasonal child workers probably did not declare an occupation to the census enumerator.

Appendix 2 Counties with the Highest Percentage of *Illiterate* Brides and Grooms in England and Wales: 1839–59

County	Average 1839–45			Average 1859		
	M (%)	F (%)	Both (%)	M (%)	F (%)	Both (%)
Monmouth	51	65	58	44	55	50
Bedfordshire	51	64	58	40	50	45
Hertfordshire	51	56	54	44	38	41
Lancashire	39	67	53	30	55	43
Worcestershire	45	60	53	30	39	35
Staffordshire	43	60	52	42	53	48
Yorkshire, W. Riding	38	64	51	26	48	37
Essex	47	53	50	37	32	35
Huntingdon	45	54	50	33	37	35
Cheshire	36	61	49	29	47	38
Buckinghamshire	43	55	49	37	39	38
Norfolk	44	50	47	36	35	36
England and Wales	33	49	41	27	38	33

Source: W. B. Stephens, *Education, Literacy and Society, 1830–70* (Manchester, 1987), pp. 322–3.

Appendix 3   Counties with the Highest Percentage of Child Employment at Ages 5–9 and 10–14: 1851 and 1871

Boys County	1851 % at work in age group	1871 % at work in age group	Girls County	1851 % at work in age group	1871 % at work in age group
			Children aged 5–9		
Bedfordshire	11.9	4.9	Bedfordshire	21.4	10.5
Hertfordshire	5.7	2.5	Buckinghamshire	11.1	3.3
Buckinghamshire	5.5	2.1	Hertfordshire	7.4	4.3
Yorkshire,			Northamptonshire	6.9	1.4
W. Riding	5.1	2.6	Leicestershire	4.9	0.9
Northamptonshire	4.3	2.2	Nottinghamshire	4.4	1.0
Leicestershire	4.1	1.0	Yorkshire,		
Nottinghamshire	3.5	0.7	W. Riding	3.7	2.7
England and Wales	*2.0*	*0.9*	*England and Wales*	*1.4*	*0.7*
			Children aged 10–14		
Yorkshire,			Bedfordshire	50.6	46.4
W. Riding	51.6	43.3	Yorkshire,		
Bedfordshire	49.6	44.4	W. Riding	35.9	28.7
Northamptonshire	47.6	45.2	Nottinghamshire	35.1	28.7
Cornwall	46.7	39.6	Buckinghamshire	34.0	27.8
Staffordshire	46.5	34.5	Derbyshire	33.8	28.7
Warwickshire	44.8	35.8	Lancashire	33.7	28.2
Buckinghamshire	44.0	39.3	Leicestershire	33.1	28.2
Lancashire	43.7	41.5	Northamptonshire	32.1	27.5
England and Wales	*36.6*	*32.1*	*England and Wales*	*19.9*	*20.5*

Source: W. B. Stephens, *Education, Literacy and Society, 1830–70* (Manchester, 1987), pp. 318–19. Order of ranking based on % of boys and girls employed in 1851.

NB: The figures undoubtedly *underestimate* the true position because of the likely undercounting of part-time, casual or seasonal workers.

Select Bibliography

Apart from the general textbooks and collections of documents, references are listed under the chapters in which they are first mentioned.

General textbooks

Cruickshank, Marjorie (1981) *Children and Industry. Child Health and Welfare in North-West Textile Towns During the Nineteenth Century* (Manchester).

Cunningham, Hugh (1991) *The Children of the Poor. Representations of Childhood Since the Seventeenth Century* (Oxford). Despite its title, this concentrates primarily upon the late eighteenth and nineteenth centuries. Concerned with society's changing perception of childhood and child labour. Uneven in its coverage of child employment but wide-ranging in its analysis.

Horn, Pamela (1990 edn) *The Victorian Country Child* (Stroud).

Nardinelli, Clark (1990) *Child Labor and the Industrial Revolution* (Bloomington and Indianapolis). Concentrates on the textile industry, although other industries are touched upon. Sees technical change rather than protective legislation as the main cause of declining child employment. Takes the view that despite its hardships factory labour was preferable for the children of the poor to other uses of their time. Presents an overoptimistic view of work in the mills but includes useful statistical tables.

Pinchbeck, Ivy and Hewitt, Margaret (1973) *Children in English Society*, vol. II: *From the Eighteenth Century to the Children Act 1948* (London). A useful survey of the main legislative changes affecting the status and employment of children over the period, but losing sight of the children themselves in the process.

Rose, Lionel (1991) *The Erosion of Childhood. Child Oppression in Britain 1860–1918* (London). Mainly covers children at work and in school. Valuable because of the breadth of juvenile employment covered, but somewhat disjointed in its presentation and lacking a clear theme.

Stephens, W. B. (1987) *Education, Literacy and Society, 1830–70: The Geography of Diversity in Provincial England* (Manchester). Analyses the interconnections between literacy levels, child employment and parental attitudes towards the education of their offspring in the mid-Victorian period. Largely concerned with the Midland and Eastern countries. Includes many useful statistical tables.

Walvin, James (1982) *A Child's World: A Social History of English Childhood 1800–1914* (Harmondsworth). A wide-ranging, somewhat superficial, survey of child life. A good introduction to the subject.

Useful collections of documents

Digby, Anne and Searby, Peter (eds) (1981) *Children, School and Society in Nineteenth Century England* (London and Basingstoke).

Pike, E. Royston (1966) *Human Documents of the Industrial Revolution in Britain* (London).

Pike, E. Royston (1967) *Human Documents of the Victorian Golden Age* (London).

Introduction 1780–1850s

Anderson, Michael (1971) *Family Structure in Nineteenth Century Lancashire* (Cambridge). A careful analysis of the life and work of families in industrial Lancashire in the mid-nineteenth century, with special reference to Preston.

Children's Employment Commission (1842) *First Report: Mining, Parliamentary Papers*, XV.

Cunningham, Hugh (1990) 'The employment and unemployment of children in England c.1680–1851', *Past and Present*, 126 (February).

Dupree, Marguerite W. (1981) Family Structure in the Staffordshire Potteries 1840–1880, Oxford University D. Phil. thesis.

Hammond, J. L. and Barbara (1949) *The Town Labourer (1760–1830)* (London: Guild Books edn).

Hartwell, R. M. (1971) *The Industrial Revolution and Economic Growth* (London).

Horn, Pamela (1978) *Education in Rural England 1800–1914* (Dublin).

Horn, Pamela (1993) 'The traffic in children and the textile mills 1780–1816', *Genealogists' Magazine*, 24, no. 5 (March).

Laqueur, Thomas (1976) *Religion and Respectability. Sunday Schools and Working Class Culture 1780–1850* (Yale).

Pollock, Linda (1988 edn) *Forgotten Children. Parent–child Relations from 1500 to 1900* (Cambridge). Sets out to test (and reject) many previously accepted views on parent–child relationships, using contemporary diaries, autobiographies and other primary sources. However, despite Pollock's diligence her sources are heavily biased towards the children of relatively well-to-do families and she is less certain in her generalizations upon the children of the lower orders.

Southey, Robert (1951) *Letters from England*, ed. Jack Simmons (London).

Thompson, E. P. (1963) *The Making of the English Working Class* (London).

Thompson, E. P. (1967) 'Time, work-discipline and industrial capitalism', *Past and Present*, 38 (December).

100

Wrigley, E. A. and Schofield, R. S. (1981) *The Population History of England 1541–1871. A Reconstruction* (London).

The impact of industrialization: 1780–1850s

Agriculture, Reports of Special Assistant Poor Law Commissioners on the Employment of Women and Children in (1843) *Parliamentary Papers*, XII.

Anderson, Michael (1976) 'Sociological history and the working-class family: Smelser revisited', *Social History*, 3 (October). Disputes Smelser's thesis (see Smelser, 1972) concerning the preservation of kinship ties in the early factories. Anderson relies upon demographic data for his analysis.

Ashton, T. S. and Sykes, J. (1929) *The Coal Industry of the Eighteenth Century* (Manchester).

Benson, J. (1970) 'The motives of 19th-century colliery owners in promoting day schools', *Journal of Educational Administration and History*, III, no. 1 (December).

Chaloner, W. H. (ed.) (1967) *The Autobiography of Samuel Bamford*, vol. 1 (London).

Children's Employment Commission, Second Report (1843) *Parliamentary Papers*, XIII and XIV.

Collier, Frances (1964) *The Family Economy of the Working Classes in the Cotton Industry 1784–1833* (Manchester).

Davies, David (1975) *The Case of Labourers in Husbandry* (London).

Dunlop, O. Jocelyn (1912) *English Apprenticeship and Child Labour* (London).

Fitton, R. S. and Wadsworth, A. P. (1958) *The Strutts and the Arkwrights* (Manchester).

Hair, P. E. H. (1982) 'Children in society 1850–1980' in Theo Barker and Michael Drake (eds), *Population and Society in Britain 1850–1980* (London).

Horn, Pamela (1974) 'Child workers in the pillow lace and straw plait trades of Victorian Buckinghamshire

101

and Bedfordshire', *Historical Journal*, XVII, no. 4 (December).

John, Angela (1980) *By the Sweat of their Brow. Women Workers at Victorian Coal Mines* (London).

Kaestle, Carl E. (ed.) (1973) *Joseph Lancaster and the Monitorial School Movement* (New York and London).

Lawson, John and Silver, Harold (1973) *A Social History of Education in England* (London).

MacKinnon, Mary and Johnson, Paul (1984) 'The case against productive whipping', *Explorations in Economic History*, 21, no. 2 (April). Strongly rejects Nardinelli's (1982) arguments below.

McKendrick, Neil (1974) 'Home demand and economic growth: A new view of the role of women and children in the Industrial Revolution' in Neil McKendrick (ed.), *Historical Perspectives. Studies in English Thought and Society* (London). This emphasizes the importance of children's earnings in contributing to the total purchasing power and hence living standards of their family.

Nardinelli, Clark (1982) 'Corporal punishment and children's wages in nineteenth century Britain', *Explorations in Economic History*, 19, no. 3 (July). Discusses the use of beating as a way of promoting child productivity and wages in industry. But see MacKinnon and Johnson (1984) above for a strong criticism of this viewpoint.

Parish Apprentices, Report of the Committee Appointed to Examine the State of (1814–15) *Parliamentary Papers*, V.

Population Census of 1851, Report of (1852–53) *Parliamentary Papers*, LXXXVIII, part I.

Rose, Mary B. (1986) *The Gregs of Quarry Bank Mill. The Rise and Decline of a Family Firm, 1750–1914* (Cambridge).

Rose, Mary B. (1989) 'Social policy and business: Parish apprenticeship and the early factory system, 1750–1834', *Business History*, 31, no. 4 (October).

Sanderson, Michael (1967) 'Education and the factory in

industrial Lancashire, 1780–1840', *Economic History Review*, 2nd Series, XX, no. 2 (August).

Sanderson, Michael (1968) 'Social change and elementary education in industrial Lancashire 1780–1840', *Northern History*, III.

Shaw, Charles (1977 edn) *When I Was a Child* (Firle).

Smelser, Neil J. (1972 edn) *Social Change in the Industrial Revolution* (London). Argues that in the early stages of factory development kinship ties were retained, as adult workers recruited their own children as their assistants. This view has now been undermined – see, for example, Anderson (1976) – but Smelser's book remains an interesting and thought-provoking text.

Turner, E. S. (1950) *Roads to Ruin* (London).

Vancouver, Charles (1808) *General Report of the Agriculture in the County of Devon* (London).

Ward, J. T. (1962) *The Factory Movement* (London). Although now somewhat dated, includes a detailed discussion of the background to the early factory legislation.

Rescue and reform: 1830–1867

Babler, Alan M. (1986) *Education of the Destitute. A Study of London Ragged Schools, 1844–1874* (Ann Arbor: University Microfilms International).

Bradlow, Edna (1984) 'The Children's Friend Society at the Cape of Good Hope', *Victorian Studies*, 27, no. 2 (Winter).

Clark, E. A. G. (1967) The Ragged School Union and the Education of the London Poor in the Nineteenth Century, London University M.Ed. thesis.

Clark, E. A. G. (1969) 'The early Ragged Schools and the foundation of the Ragged School Union', *Journal of Educational Administration and History*, I, no. 2 (June).

Clark, E. A. G. (1988) 'The diffusion of educational ideas: The case of Ragged and Industrial Schools', *Journal of*

Educational Administration and History, XX, no. 1 (January).

Clarke, Allen (1985 edn) *The Effects of the Factory System* (Littleborough).

Cowan, I. D. (1984) 'Certified industrial training ships c. 1860–1913', *Journal of Educational Administration and History*, XVI, no. 1 (January).

Criminal and Destitute Juveniles, Select Committee on (1852) *Parliamentary Papers*, VII. Evidence of Mr William Locke, honorary secretary of the London Ragged School Union.

Crowther, M. A. (1978) *The Workhouse System 1834–1929. The History of an English Social Institution* (Athens, Georgia).

Digby, Anne (1978) *Pauper Palaces* (London).

Duke, Francis (1976) 'Pauper education' in Derek Fraser (ed.), *The New Poor Law in the Nineteenth Century* (London and Basingstoke).

Eden, Sir Frederic Morton, Bart. (1966 edn) *The State of the Poor*, vol. 2 (London). This is a facsimile of the original 1797 edition.

Education of Destitute Children, Select Committee on the (1861) *Parliamentary Papers*, VII. Evidence of Mr J. G. Gent and Mr William Locke.

Factories and Workshops (1872) *Reports under the Laws relating to, for the half-year ended 30 April, 1872. Report by Robert Baker, Parliamentary Papers*, XVI.

Floud, Roderick and Wachter, Kenneth W. (1982) 'Poverty and physical stature. Evidence on the standard of living of London boys 1770–1870', *Social Science History*, 6, no. 4 (Fall).

Forsythe, W. J. (1983) *A System of Discipline. Exeter Borough Prison 1819–1863* (Exeter).

Frostick, Elizabeth (1990) *The Story of Hull and its People* (Hull).

Frow, Edmund and Ruth (1970) *The Half-time System in Education* (Manchester).

Hadley, Elaine (1990) 'Natives in a strange land: The philanthropic discourse of juvenile emigration in mid-nineteenth-century England', *Victorian Studies*, 33, no. 3 (Spring). A valuable analysis of the ambiguous attitudes displayed by philanthropists in their dealings with destitute children.

Horner, Leonard (1840) *On the Employment of Children in Factories and Other Works in the United Kingdom* (London).

May, Margaret (1973) 'Innocence and experience: The evolution of the concept of juvenile delinquency in the mid-nineteenth century', *Victorian Studies*, XVIII, no. 1 (September).

Mayhew, Henry (1968 edn) *London Labour and the London Poor*, vol. I (New York).

Melling, Elizabeth (ed.) (1964) *Kentish Sources. IV: The Poor* (Maidstone).

Nardinelli, Clark (1980) 'Child labor and the Factory Acts', *Journal of Economic History*, XL, no. 4 (December).

Population Census for 1871, Report of (1873) *Parliamentary Papers*, LXXI, part II.

Reformatory and Industrial Schools (1871) *Thirteenth Annual Report of, Parliamentary Papers*, XXXVI.

Rose, June (1987) *For the Sake of the Children. Inside Dr. Barnardo's: 120 Years of Caring for Children* (London).

Silver, Harold (1977) 'Ideology and the factory child: Attitudes to half-time education' in P. McCann (ed.), *Popular Education and Socialization in the Nineteenth Century* (London).

Stack, J. A. (1982) 'Interests and ideas in nineteenth century social policy: The mid-Victorian Reformatory School', *Journal of Educational Administration and History*, XIV, no. 1 (January).

Tobias, J. J. (1967) *Crime and Industrial Society in the Nineteenth Century* (London).

Wagner, Gillian (1982) *Children of the Empire* (London).

Ward, Gertrude (1935) 'The education of factory child workers, 1833–1850. A study of the effects of the educational clauses in the Factory Act of 1833', *Economic History*, 3 (February).

Behlmer, George K. (1982) *Child Abuse and Moral Reform in England, 1870–1908* (Stanford, California). An important survey of the background to late-Victorian reforms concerned to protect children against cruelty and which led to the establishment of the National Society for the Prevention of Cruelty to Children in 1889. Deals with a generally neglected theme.

Education: Reports on Schools for the Poorer Classes in the Municipal Boroughs of Birmingham, Leeds, Liverpool and Manchester in 1869 (1870) *Parliamentary Papers*, LIV. Some of the material included in these reports was used by W. E. Forster to justify the need for the 1870 Elementary Education Act. But see West (1975) below for a critical examination of the findings of the reports.

Final Report of the School Board for London 1870–1904 (1904) (London).

Hansard, 3rd Series, vol. 194 (December 1868–March 1869), cols 1194–95 for speech by George Melly, MP; vol. 199 (February–March 1870), cols 438, 442 and 465–6 for speech by W. E. Forster, MP.

Horn, Pamela (1989) *The Victorian and Edwardian Schoolchild* (Gloucester).

Hurt, J. S. (1979) *Elementary Schooling and the Working Classes 1860–1918* (London). Concerned with the social, economic and educational problems which lay behind the efforts to impose compulsory schooling in the later years of the nineteenth century.

Hurt, J. S. (1988) *Outside the Mainstream. A History of Special Education* (London).

Keeling, Frederic (1914) *Child Labour in the United Kingdom* (London).

London Society for the Prevention of Cruelty to Children (1887) *Third Report* (London).

Middleton, Nigel (1970) 'The Education Act of 1870 as the start of the modern concept of the child', *British Journal of Educational Studies*, 18.

Pritchard, D. G. (1963) *Education and the Handicapped 1760–1960* (London).

Reeves, John (1913) *Recollections of a School Attendance Officer* (London).

Rose, Lionel (1986) *The Massacre of the Innocents. Infanticide in Britain 1800–1939* (London).

Rubinstein, David (1969) *School Attendance in London, 1870–1904: A Social History* (Hull).

School Board for London: Meals for School Children. Report of a Special Sub-Committee of the School Management Committee (1889) (Greater London Record Office, SBL.1467).

Stafford, Ann (1964) *The Age of Consent* (London).

West, E. G. (1975) *Education and the Industrial Revolution* (London).

Conclusion: the working-class child in the 1880s

Hendrick, Harry (1990) *Images of Youth. Age, Class, and the Male Youth Problem, 1880–1920* (Oxford).

Hendrick, Harry (1992) *Children and Childhood* (University of York: *Refresh*, no. 15, Autumn).

Searle, G. R. (1976) *Eugenics and Politics in Britain 1900–14* (Leyden).

Index

110